ENERGY

Model of Hero's
aeolipile, c. AD 100

Bell's box telephone, 1886-1887

Hampson air liquifier,
mid 20th century

Early mariner's
compass

Late 19th-century
kerosene lamp

Heating coal to
produce coal gas

DK EYEWITNESS BOOKS

ENERGY

Written by
JACK CHALLONER

Late 19th-century
burning lens

Late 19th-century apparatus
to show that heat causes
expansion in solids

Model of a Greek ship of 800 BC

Model of an early
20th-century tram

L.C.C.

Model of a Pelton wheel,
late 19th century

Melting ice in
a hot liquid

Dorling Kindersley

Late 19th-century electricity meter

Dorling Kindersley
LONDON, NEW YORK, AUCKLAND, DELHI,
JOHANNESBURG, MUNICH, PARIS and SYDNEY

For a full catalog, visit
DK www.dk.com

Model of
Huygens's
pendulum
timepiece of 1673

Project editor Stephanie Jackson
Art editor Gurinder Purewall
Designer Marianna Papachrysanthou
Production Eunice Paterson
Managing editor Josephine Buchanan
Senior art editor Thomas Keenes
Picture research Deborah Pownall,
Catherine O'Rourke
Special photography Clive Streeter
Editorial consultant Brian Bowers,
Science Museum, London
US editor Charles A. Wills
US consultant Professor Warren Yasso
Teachers College, Columbia University

This Eyewitness ® Book has been conceived by
Dorling Kindersley Limited and Editions Gallimard

© 1993 Dorling Kindersley Limited
This edition © 2000 Dorling Kindersley Limited
First American edition, 1993

Published in the United States by
Dorling Kindersley Publishing, Inc.
95 Madison Avenue
New York, NY 10016
4 6 8 10 9 7 5 3

Dorling Kindersley books are available at special discounts for bulk purchases for sales
promotions or premiums. Special editions, including personalized covers, excerpts of
existing guides, and corporate imprints can be created in large quantities for specific
needs. For more information, contact Special Markets Dept., Dorling Kindersley
Publishing, Inc., 95 Madison Ave., New York, NY 10016; Fax: (800) 600-9098

Library of Congress Cataloging–in–Publication Data
Challoner, Jack.
Energy / written by Jack Challoner.
p. cm. — (Eyewitness Books)
Includes index.
Summary: Surveys various sources of energy and the ways in which they have
been harnessed.
1. Power resources — Juvenile literature.
[1. Power resources. 2. Force and energy.]
I. Title. II. Series.
TJ163.23.C43   2000
621.042 — dc20   92-54479
                                                CIP
                                                AC

ISBN 0-7894-6191-9 (pb)
ISBN 0-7894-5576-5 (hc)

Late 19th-century thermometer

Boys's gas
calorimeter, early
20th century

Color reproduction by Colourscan, Singapore
Printed in China by Toppan Printing Co. (Shenzhen) Ltd.

Contents

Model of Egyptian
seagoing boat,
c. 1300 BC

What is energy?

WITHOUT ENERGY, there would be nothing. There would be no Sun, no wind, no rivers, and no life at all. Energy is everywhere, and energy changing from one form to another is behind everything that happens. Energy, defined as the ability to make things happen, cannot be created. Nor can it be destroyed. Plants and animals harness energy from nature to help them grow and survive. The most intelligent of animals, human beings, have developed many ways of using the available energy to improve their lives. Ancient people used energy from fire (pp. 10–11), and they developed tools to use energy from their muscles (pp. 8–9) more effectively. But ancient people did not understand the role of energy in their lives. Such an understanding of energy has really developed only over the past few hundred years.

THE FAITHFUL SUN
The Sun (pp. 48-49) is the supplier of nearly all the energy on Earth. The energy from the Sun travels through the 93 million miles (150 million km) of space to the Earth as electromagnetic radiation (pp. 40-41), a form of energy that includes light, X-rays, and radio waves.

AN ENERGETIC FROG
This frog needs energy to jump. Because anything that moves has energy (pp. 16-17), energy is needed to start the frog moving. The frog obtains the energy it needs from food (pp. 52-53). When the frog lands, it will lose the energy of its movement. But the energy will still exist as heat (pp. 20-21) in its body and in the surrounding soil, air, and water.

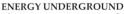

ENERGY UNDERGROUND
The energy released by this geyser did not come from the Sun. It comes from the heat of molten rock in the Earth and heat generated by friction and pressure as the rocks deep underground push against each other. In some places, people use the heat energy generated in this way as an alternative to fossil fuels (pp. 54-55) for heating homes or generating electricity (pp. 58-59).

A BRIGHT SPARK
On a hot and humid day, electrical energy builds up as electric charges separate in the clouds. When the separation is large enough, there is enough energy to spark from the cloud down to the ground in an impressive display. The electrical energy becomes heat energy, light energy, and the sound energy of thunder.

SEETHING VOLCANO
Huge amounts of energy are released in a large volcanic eruption. This painting of the eruption of Mount Vesuvius in Italy shows molten lava, smoke, poisonous gas, and ashes being blown into the air. In AD 79, the volcano erupted, covering the towns of Herculaneum and Pompeii with debris.

CARNIVOROUS PLANT
Animals need to obtain
their energy by eating other
living things. But most plants
can store energy directly from the Sun
by a process called photosynthesis (pp. 50-51).
When sunlight falls on a plant, it causes chemical
reactions which result in energy being stored in
chemicals within the plant. Some plants, such as this
Venus fly trap, supplement their energy by attracting
insects – they digest the insects, making use of the
energy and chemicals stored in the insect's body.

ENERGY FROM THE WIND
Energy is needed to make these trees bend over. As the Sun
heats the Earth, it does so unevenly, because some parts of
the Earth heat up more quickly than others. This causes
differences in air pressure, and high-pressure air moves to
equalize with lower-pressure air, creating winds. So the
energy from wind (pp. 12-13) is really energy from the Sun.

ENERGY IN RUNNING WATER
As the Sun's energy warms the seas
and rivers, some of the water evaporates,
and it rises high into the atmosphere
where it condenses to form clouds. The
water droplets in the clouds gather
and fall back to Earth as raindrops.
The rain gathers into fast-moving
streams (pp. 12-13). The energy
of running water comes
originally from the Sun.

Muscle energy

IN ANCIENT TIMES, PEOPLE USED THE ENERGY of their own muscles to do work such as gathering food and building shelter. To make this muscle energy even more useful, and to use it efficiently, early people invented simple tools. The first tools were made of wood and stone, but once smelting was developed (pp. 10-11) metal tools became available. Another source of muscle power was found in animals – one large animal, such as an ox, can be up to seven times more powerful than one human. Animals were used on their own for transporting people and goods, but they were also used together with simple tools and machines to perform more complex tasks, such as plowing fields and pumping water for irrigation. By making more use of this kind of muscle energy, people had more time to develop other skills and activities.

Wall painting from the tomb of the Pharaoh Rekmire showing an Egyptian bow drill in use

Bow

Leather string makes the pole rotate

Central pole

Metal tip

INUIT ENERGY SAVER
One of the earliest types of tool is the bow drill. Bow drills were used in many cultures for jobs as varied as starting fires (pp. 10-11) and drilling holes. This Inuit bow drill was probably made for drilling holes in bones and wood. Bow drills are made from a central pole, which is held firmly in place but can rotate, and a bow that quickly rotates the central pole. This action transfers the human muscle energy to the tip of the central pole, where the work is being done.

PLOWING THE SOIL
A plow is a tool used to break up soil to prepare it for sowing seeds. This model, showing a man driving a plow pulled by a pair of oxen, was found buried deep in an Egyptian tomb of c. 2000 BC. It shows that people have used plows for thousands of years. In fact, the first plows were used around 4000 BC in Mesopotamia. Originally, they were pushed entirely by people, but later people learned to make plows more efficient by using animals that pulled a plow as it was pushed into the soil by a person.

Person applies muscle energy to the plow

The tip of the plow breaks the soil

Plow is pushed into soil

SADDLE STONE GRINDER
Grinding grain was one of the major activities of early peoples. Many machines have been used to supply the energy for this task, including windmills and water wheels (pp. 12-13), steam engines (pp. 28-29), and electric motors. The earliest method involved placing the grain on a stone, called a saddle stone because of its shape, and crushing the grains with another stone, which was often called a rubber. This Egyptian limestone figure of c. 2310 BC was found in a tomb. It shows a female servant grinding grain and suggests that this was a common activity as long as 4,000 years ago.

Soil

Stern, or rear, of boat

Rowers sat on these seats

Bow, or front, of boat

Steering oar

Oars were rowed using the muscle energy of the slaves

MAKING THE MOST OF OTHER PEOPLE'S ENERGY

Some people used their authority to exploit other people's energy for their own benefit. This is a model of a Greek ship from about 800 BC. The ship was powered by the muscle energy of a team of slaves. One Roman galley was said to have had 4,000 slaves at the oars. The use of oarsmen to power ships in this way died out by the 18th century as better rigging made it possible to power large ships using the wind.

Greenstone blade can cut and chop

Grass rope binds the ax together

Viking ship using human muscle energy and wind energy (pp. 12-13)

The yoke is fastened to the oxen so they can pull the plow

The plow is fastened to the yoke

Wooden handle

Two oxen are used to pull the plow

PRIMITIVE HAND AX

There were many tasks for primitive peoples, such as killing animals for food, that required a heavy blow with a sharp object. Muscle energy is needed to move a hand ax through the air. As the ax strikes an object, for example, a block of wood, this energy is transferred to the object and can do useful work, such as chopping wood. This type of ax, from Papua New Guinea, is still used for general woodwork.

Energy from fire

MYTHS ABOUT FIRE
The energy released by burning fuels was an extremely important resource for early people. But even though fire was used every day, they did not understand what it really was. To them, fire was magic. Throughout the world, different cultures had different ideas to explain where fire came from. Some said it was given by the gods. This statue is of Xuihtecuhtli, the Aztec Lord of Fire. His image was placed in the hearth of every Aztec home.

HUMAN BEINGS HAVE USED FIRE for thousands of years, though the date of the discovery or first use of fire is unknown. It is known, however, that late Stone Age cave dwellers kept their caves warm with fires which, it seems, were kept alight continuously for months or years. Since then, people have learned to use the energy of fire in many ways, from cooking food and lighting their homes, to smelting ore, firing pottery, and making glass. Most of the energy from fire is heat energy (pp. 20-21) that is released when a fuel is burned. The first fuel was wood, but charcoal, which is produced by heating wood without air, burns with a hotter flame. Burning charcoal and using bellows to increase the supply of air causes the charcoal to burn hotter, making it possible to extract metals from their ores. The metal atoms in metal ores are usually bound tightly to oxygen atoms, and energy from fire is needed to separate them into oxygen plus the pure metal. Although most of the energy of fire is heat, energy in the form of light and sound is also released. This is why fire can be seen, felt, and heard.

FIRE FOR COOKING
There is evidence from caves in China that fire was first used in cooking as long ago as 500,000 years. The heat energy from fire can be used to change food in many ways. It can make meat more tender, and it can make food safer to eat by killing harmful bacteria. Also, the heat of a fire can help combine ingredients into new substances, as it does when dough is baked into bread.

SMELTING THE ORE
Ores are rocks that contain metals, but not in a pure state. Energy is needed to extract, or "smelt," metals from their ores. The metal atoms are tightly combined with atoms of other elements, such as oxygen. The energy that fire supplies breaks the metal from its bonds with the other elements. The first metals to be smelted were copper and tin, which people later learned to combine to make bronze. All metals need a high temperature to be smelted, and the use of bellows helps to reach this by increasing the supply of air to the fire. This is a model of a primitive hearth from the Sudan in Africa. A hearth like this one can reach temperatures of around 1650° F (900° C). In some parts of Central Africa, smelting hearths are still used.

Sticks operate the bellows

Bellows increase the supply of air to the fire

Charcoal is the fuel for the fire

Metal ore is placed in the fire

Smelted metal is left at the bottom of the fire

Upper level is cooler

Ceramic pots held the batch for melting

Containers for cooling glass slowly

Blowpipe was inserted through one of these windows

Wood fire is burned at the bottom of the furnace

GLASSMAKER'S FURNACE

Fire is an essential element in making glass. The main ingredient of glass is sand, which is mixed with other ingredients to form the "batch." The batch is melted by the heat from fire; and when it is cooled the glass is formed. A fire raged at the bottom of this 16th-century furnace, and the batch was melted in the large ceramic pots. A glass blower could then reach through one of the windows and pick up some of the molten mixture on the end of a "blowpipe," which was then used to blow the glass into the desired shape. A mold could also be used to help achieve this. Glass was first made as long ago as 4000 BC, and there is evidence to show that it was blown in this way during the 1st century BC.

ROMAN CENTRAL HEATING

Fire has been used to heat homes for many thousands of years. The ancient Greeks were the first to use central heating, but the Romans improved on it with a sophisticated heating system called a "hypocaust." It heated the rooms of public baths and some houses. A fire was lit and tended by a slave, and the hot air from the fire moved around in ducts under the floors, eventually escaping through a chimney. This potentially dangerous use of fire in the home may have been one of the reasons the Romans were also the first to have organized fire fighters.

Roman glass bottles, c. AD 3-4

Bellows are made of leather and clay

Energy from wind and water

ANCIENT PEOPLE COULD SEE that there was tremendous force in the natural motion of wind and water. Although they had no scientific understanding of energy, they realized they could harness these natural forces to do some heavy work. Early civilizations used "mechanical energy" to do work like lifting, grinding grain, building, and transporting people and goods (pp. 8-9). This mechanical energy could be obtained from wind or moving water. Wind and water flow are the most visible examples of natural energy on the Earth, but that energy originally comes from the Sun (pp. 48-49). The wind that turns the sails of a windmill and fills the sails of a sailing boat is caused by the Sun heating the Earth. The rain that falls from the sky was once ocean, lake, or river water that evaporated back into the atmosphere because of the Sun's energy.

ENERGY FOR THE DAILY GRIND
Horizontal water wheels like this are called "Greek" or "Norse" wheels. This wheel was used to grind grain into flour. Grain was placed into the top of the funnel-shaped container, called a hopper, and fell down between the millstones. The top millstone was turned by the water wheel underneath, and the grain was crushed to make flour, which fell down into the trough below. Horizontal wheels like this need fast-moving water to be effective.

Water power

Water wheels were used for irrigation as long ago as 600 BC, but water power was first used for grinding corn around 100 BC in various parts of the world. The type of water wheel used depended on how fast the stream or river flowed. The use of water power has since developed in many different ways, and it is still an important alternative to fossil fuels (pp. 58-59).

Gears transfer mechanical energy to different parts of the mill

Belts are attached to pulleys

Reels hold the cotton

USING WATER IN INDUSTRY
Until the invention of the steam engine (pp. 28-29), water power was heavily used in industry. This model shows a cotton mill that was built at the end of the 18th century. Water flowed underneath the mill, turning the water wheel. The movement of the water was a reliable and free source of energy. It powered the machines in the mill through gears and pulleys. To make use of water, such mills had to be built near rivers. Steam engines, in contrast, could be used anywhere – one of the main reasons steam power took over in industry.

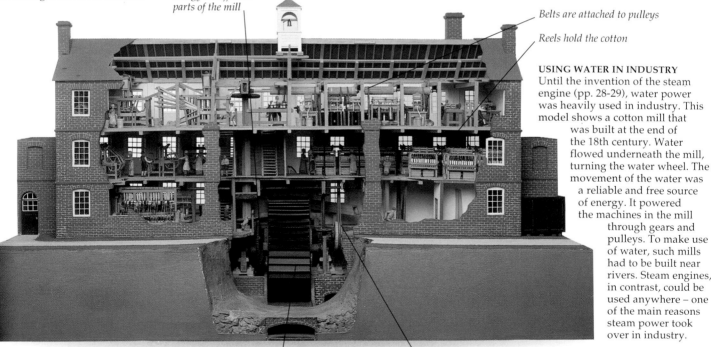

The wheel moves in the direction of the water flow

Water falls into the water wheel

Undershot water wheel

Belts transmit the power from the water wheel to the machines

OVERSHOT WHEEL
Overshot water wheels are used where water falls from a great height, having potential energy (pp. 14-15), but is slow moving, having little kinetic energy (pp. 16-17). The water pulls one side of the wheel around with it as the water falls.

Slow-moving water source

UNDERSHOT WHEEL
These water wheels are used in fast-moving water, which has a lot of kinetic energy (pp. 16-17). The water passes under the wheel and pushes blades, which turn the wheel. This could be connected to heavy machinery in factories.

The wheel moves in the direction of the water flow

Fast-moving water source

Wind power

One of the earliest forms of power that people learned to use, wind was used to move boats with cloth sails as long ago as 3500 BC. On land, the first windmills seem to have been used in Persia around AD 700. The sails turned horizontally and were connected directly to grindstones used to grind grain. Wind power is also used for irrigating dry land and draining wet land. The wind is used as an alternative energy source to generate electricity.

The vanes turn at a constant speed, even if the wind speed changes

This mechanism allows each sail or vane to twist automatically away from the wind, if the wind is too strong

Large hopper directs the grain onto the grindstone

Large gear wheel transmits power to the grindstone

Top cap houses the machinery that takes the motion of the sails and converts it into the mechanical energy of the grindstone

Fantail regulates the movement of the top cap

Top cap turns automatically, so the sails face the wind if the fantail turns

Mast holds the sail

Square sail captures the wind

Oars are used to steer the boat

Animal carvings decorate covered seats

Grindstone grinds the corn

Balcony

Living quarters for the miller

Early 19th-century windmill

GRINDING CORN
This is a model of a windmill built at the beginning of the 19th century in the UK. Like most European mills, it has vertical (rather than horizontal) sails or vanes. They turn around as some of the horizontal motion of the wind is changed to a rotational motion of the sails. Their motion is transferred by gears and pulleys to a grindstone, which grinds grain into flour. To make use of as much of the energy of the wind as possible, the "top cap" of the windmill automatically turns around to face into the wind if the wind changes direction. Wind power is of great importance in places prone to flooding, like Holland, where it has been used for pumping water to drain the land. In 1341, a bishop in Holland even tried to claim legally all of the wind that blew through his town.

SAILING BOATS
Most modern sailboats have triangular sails that can be moved to catch the most wind energy. This is a model of an Egyptian ship from around 1300 BC that used square sails, which can efficiently use the energy of the wind only if they have the wind behind them. By 200 BC, ships in the Mediterranean used sails that could be moved to make use of the wind's energy, even if it was not blowing directly behind the sails.

LISTENING TO THE WIND
The Greek engineer Hero of Alexandria (pp. 28-29) designed this musical organ which was powered by the wind. Sound (pp. 40-41) is a form of energy that travels from the source to our ears by the vibration of air molecules. Hero used the energy of the wind to push a piston in the organ back and forth. The piston pushed air through the organ pipes, which vibrated the air around them, making the sound. Hero's design for this organ is very similar to the design of the modern pipe organ.

Potential energy

AN EGG THAT IS RELEASED from some height on to a hard surface will fall, and it will probably break. Before the egg is released, it has the "potential" to fall. People know that an egg released from a height will fall, and most people also realize that the higher and the heavier the egg, the greater the chance that it will break. But where does the egg's potential to fall come from? Someone may have lifted it up, working against gravity and using the energy in their muscles from the food they have eaten (pp. 52-53) to do so. Potential energy is stored whenever something moves in the opposite direction to a force acting on it. So, stretching an elastic band stores energy because the molecules of the elastic are moved apart, working against the forces between the molecules that are pulling them together. There are many forms of potential energy, and many forms of energy that it can become. But the total amount of energy always stays the same (pp. 24-25).

The hands turn slowly with the release of energy from the falling weight

HUYGENS'S CLOCK
Dutch scientist Christian Huygens (1629-1695) was the inventor of the pendulum clock, which he first devised by attaching a pendulum to the gears of a mechanical clock. The regular swing of the pendulum made the clock run much more precisely than before. This is a model of a clock Huygens made in 1673. The energy to drive the hands of this clock against friction comes from the falling of the lead weight, which releases a fraction of the weight's potential energy with each tick. The clock stops when the weight reaches its lowest position. The energy, or "work," of the person who raises the weight is stored in the weight as potential energy, which is released as the weight descends.

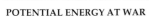

POTENTIAL ENERGY AT WAR
These Roman soldiers are storing their muscle energy in a catapult. When the catapult is released, the potential energy the soldiers contributed is released. The catapult will shoot a missile forward toward the enemy, using all of its stored potential energy.

Small weight acts as a counter-balance, keeping the string tight

Lead weight loses potential energy as it descends

WINDING UP THE CLOCK
Inside a mechanical clock is a coiled piece of metal called a "mainspring." The mainspring stores the muscle energy of the person who winds up the clock. The clock can run for a few days by releasing the potential energy stored in the mainspring. This clock mechanism transforms this energy into the movement of the hands, the sound of the ticking, and a small amount of heat (pp. 20-21). Many other types of clock, such as water clocks or candle clocks, rely on the steady release of some form of potential energy to keep time. Many scientists used to think the Universe was like a huge clockwork machine, gradually winding down as time passes.

GRANDFATHER CLOCK
A "grandfather clock" is a large clock that is housed in a freestanding case. This one has three dials, all driven by the energy of the falling weights.

Key is used to transfer energy from the muscles to the clock

Gearing inside the clock mechanism controls the release of the energy

The pendulum is kept swinging by the energy of the falling weight

STUDYING IMPACT

Although it was not until the mid-19th century that people really understood potential energy, it was the subject of many experiments carried out during the century before. In this experiment Dutch scientist Willem s'Gravesande (pp. 16-17) studied potential energy by dropping balls of various weights on to soft clay. He found that the impact the balls made in the clay depended on the weight of the balls and the height from which the balls fell. In other words, the potential of the balls to make an impact was greater for heavier balls and for those dropped from a greater height. S'Gravesande also experimented with the energy stored in springs, and he built machines to measure and demonstrate the properties of moving objects.

Metal ball

ENERGY IN A MATCH HEAD

A match stores potential energy in the chemicals that form the match head. Many chemicals, or mixtures of chemicals, undergo reactions in which they may give out energy. When a match is rubbed against a scratchy surface, the molecules in the head of the match are rearranged. The molecules react by igniting, causing energy to be released in the form of heat (pp. 20-21) and light.

Chemicals in the match head store potential energy

Scratchy surface against which the match is rubbed

When the match is struck, it ignites

Soft clay records the impact of the ball

The size of the dent can now be measured

The ball has used its potential energy to make the dent

1 POTENTIAL ENERGY

The metal ball is suspended over some soft clay. The ball has been weighed beforehand, and now its height over the clay is measured. In order to release the potential energy stored in the ball, the string must be cut.

2 THE ENERGY OF IMPACT

The impact in the clay shows the amount of kinetic energy (pp. 16-17) of the ball as it hit the clay. The kinetic energy of an object increases as it accelerates. If the ball had twice the weight, it would have had twice the impact.

GALILEO GALILEI

One of the first modern physicists was Galileo Galilei (1564-1642), an Italian scholar. He experimented with objects falling and rolling down slopes. Although he could not have known about energy, he seemed to have a natural grasp of the idea of potential energy. This was truly remarkable because, at the time, everyone else followed the ideas of Aristotle (pp. 16-17), who thought that objects moved because it was "in their nature to do so." By combining careful experimentation and brilliant reasoning, Galileo showed that this view was incorrect. Objects fall not just because they are heavy, but because they are given potential energy – perhaps by someone lifting them. Without Galileo, it may have taken much longer to realize this.

The barrel has potential energy

To make use of its potential energy, the barrel must be pushed over the "hill"

The barrel has used its supply of potential energy

POTENTIAL HILL

Energy is needed to move any object against the force of gravity, which tries to pull the object down. To get a barrel to the top of a hill, muscle energy must be applied to move the barrel. When the barrel rolls down the hill, it gradually loses its potential energy until it reaches its lowest potential energy at the bottom of the slope. Natural processes act in the same way, always finding their lowest energy. Notice the shape of the hill: it has a bump over which the barrel must be pushed before its potential energy can be released. Many chemical reactions, like the burning of matches (see top), also have a potential energy "hill" – they must be given energy to start, but then they continue of their own accord. For matches, the energy to get over the hill is supplied by the heat produced when the matches are struck.

The energy of movement

Everything that moves has energy called "kinetic" energy. The faster an object moves, and the more mass it has, the more kinetic energy it has. In 1686, the German mathematician Gottfried Wilhelm Leibniz (1646-1716) introduced the term *vis viva*, meaning living force, which was very close to the idea of kinetic energy that was worked out in the 1800s. The *vis viva* of an object depended on its mass and speed. Scientists noticed that this energy seemed to be "conserved" – a moving ball could transfer its energy to a stationary one. However, when a moving object hits a soft material, such as sand, it is obvious that the energy is not conserved because the sand seems to absorb the movement. This puzzle remained unsolved until it was shown that moving objects have energy that can be changed into other forms (pp. 24-25). Thus, when a moving object hits sand the energy is not lost, but changed into a form such as heat. All forms of energy are either kinetic or potential energy (pp.14-15).

WHAT THE GREEKS THOUGHT
The Greek philosopher Aristotle (384-322 BC) thought that things move towards their "natural place" because of their nature. A stone is heavy, so it will fall. It is in a bird's nature to fly. Because these ideas seemed correct, no one tested them to find out whether they were true. Indeed, it was nearly 2,000 years later that people started experimenting with objects in motion and challenging Aristotle's view.

Moving hammer has a lot of kinetic energy

The kinetic energy of the hammer is transferred to the nail

HAMMERING THE NAIL
The head of a hammer has a good deal of kinetic energy as it strikes a nail. Once the hammer comes to a stop it has lost all of its kinetic energy. But the energy has not disappeared. It has been transferred to the atoms and molecules of the nail, the wood, the air, and even the hammer. This random kinetic energy is heat (pp.20-21).

The energy the nail gains is transferred to the wood

Two objects of the same mass

SAME MASS, DIFFERENT SPEEDS *(left and above)*
Two objects of the same mass traveling at different speeds have different amounts of kinetic energy. A ball with twice the speed will have four times the kinetic energy. Kinetic energy depends on the square of the speed (four is two squared). A ball with ten times the speed will have 100 times the kinetic energy.

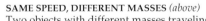

Two objects of different masses

SAME SPEED, DIFFERENT MASSES *(above)*
Two objects with different masses traveling at the same speed have different amounts of kinetic energy. An object with twice the mass will have twice the kinetic energy. The mass of an object is the amount of matter it is made of, and mass is directly related to weight, which is the force of gravity pulling on an object.

SCIENTISTS IN CONFLICT
Through the 18th century, there was a great deal of argument about Leibniz's idea of *vis viva*. One person involved in this controversy was Gabrielle de Breteuil, Marquise du Châtelet (c. 1700-1749). Many scientists rejected the idea of *vis viva*, but the Marquise was convinced that Leibniz was right. In 1740 she wrote a book that convinced many others that the *vis viva* idea was correct.

STUDYING *VIS VIVA*
Dutch scientist Willem s'Gravesande (1688-1742) built several machines to experiment with motion. He also made machines that calculated how compressed springs can make things move as they are released. It seemed that the *vis viva* was somehow stored up in the spring. It is now known that potential energy (pp. 14-15) stored in an object, such as a spring, becomes kinetic energy as it makes an object move.

Balls are suspended from pegs

EXPERIMENTING WITH COLLISIONS
This replica of one of s'Gravesande's machines has two balls. One ball is made to swing from a particular distance from the middle of the apparatus and collide with the other, stationary, ball. The masses of the balls and the distances that they swing are measured. S'Gravesande used this information to calculate how much *vis viva* the moving ball had at the time of collision. Although Leibniz believed that the total amount of *vis viva* stayed the same, the balls eventually came to a stop. Leibniz suggested that the motion was not lost, but became motion inside the ball. We now know that this motion is heat (pp. 20-21).

FIRING A BULLET
Whenever something is made to move, it is given kinetic energy. When a bullet is fired, the energy for the movement of the bullet comes from the explosion of gunpowder in the barrel. The explosion produces mainly heat energy. This is transferred to the air in the gun barrel, which rapidly expands as it is heated, giving its kinetic energy to the bullet. The bullet is pushed at high speed, and the energy of the bullet is then transferred to the object the bullet hits.

Pegs mark the positions of the strings

Scale allows distance of ball from the center of the machine to be measured

Stationary ball is hit by moving ball

Ball is released from a particular distance

Imponderable fluids

M OST SCIENTISTS of the 18th century believed that matter is made of particles. Many of them thought that effects such as light, heat, magnetism, and electricity were also made of particles. These "effects" were known to travel from place to place. Scientists thought that to do this, the particles had to flow like fluid, be weightless (experiments to weigh heat and electricity were unsuccessful), and be able to penetrate objects. Each phenomenon was thought to be carried by different fluids, which were called "imponderable fluids," so they would be completely separate. The greatest interest was in heat (pp. 20-21) and electricity (pp. 22-23); further study of these effects contributed to the downfall of this theory. By the middle of the 19th century the idea of imponderable fluids was proven to be incorrect (pp. 20-21).

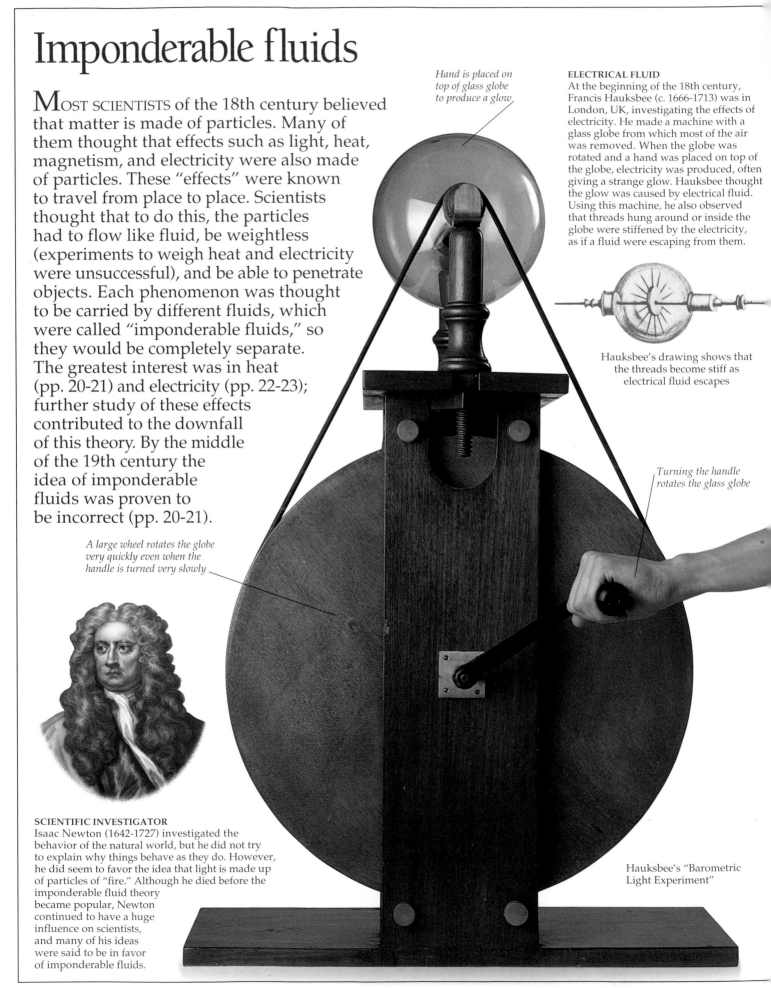

Hand is placed on top of glass globe to produce a glow

ELECTRICAL FLUID
At the beginning of the 18th century, Francis Hauksbee (c. 1666-1713) was in London, UK, investigating the effects of electricity. He made a machine with a glass globe from which most of the air was removed. When the globe was rotated and a hand was placed on top of the globe, electricity was produced, often giving a strange glow. Hauksbee thought the glow was caused by electrical fluid. Using this machine, he also observed that threads hung around or inside the globe were stiffened by the electricity, as if a fluid were escaping from them.

Hauksbee's drawing shows that the threads become stiff as electrical fluid escapes

Turning the handle rotates the glass globe

A large wheel rotates the globe very quickly even when the handle is turned very slowly

SCIENTIFIC INVESTIGATOR
Isaac Newton (1642-1727) investigated the behavior of the natural world, but he did not try to explain why things behave as they do. However, he did seem to favor the idea that light is made up of particles of "fire." Although he died before the imponderable fluid theory became popular, Newton continued to have a huge influence on scientists, and many of his ideas were said to be in favor of imponderable fluids.

Hauksbee's "Barometric Light Experiment"

RING AND BALL

During the 18th century, scientific demonstrations became very popular. One reason so many people supported the imponderable fluid theory was that it seemed to explain their observations. In one famous demonstration, a cold metal ball that just fitted through a ring would not fit through the same ring after the ball was heated. This was explained by the idea that heat is a fluid made of particles, which entered the ball and made it bigger.

The ring is movable and passes easily over the ball

Particle of matter

Particle of fluid

Fluid passing between objects

Matter with high fluid concentration   Matter with low fluid concentration

FLUID MADE OF PARTICLES OF FIRE

Many people thought the fluids carrying light, electricity, and heat were made of particles of fire. Heat fluid is hot, light is given off by hot objects, and electricity makes hot sparks. The particles of these fluids penetrated between the particles of matter, and they pushed each other and the matter particles apart. Fluid could pass between objects containing more or less concentrated fluid.

This could explain why hot objects lost their heat to colder ones, for example.

The ring is moved away, so that it will not get hot

The flame of the bunsen burner heats the ball

The metal has been tarnished by the flame

The ball has expanded and the ring no longer passes over it

1 SMALL BALL
In the first stage of this experiment, the ball is cold, and the ring passes easily over it. The ball is a solid, and it is composed of millions of closely packed particles.

2 ADDING FLUID
The ball is heated by a hot flame. Particles of heat fluid were thought to pass from the flame into the ball. The hotter the ball becomes, the more heat fluid it contains.

3 FILLED WITH FLUID
The ball has expanded so much that the ring cannot pass over it. It was thought that particles of the metal were pushed apart as particles of heat fluid were crammed between them.

ELECTRICAL FLUID

American scientist Benjamin Franklin (1706-1790) is famous for demonstrating that lightning is electrical. He flew a kite in a thunderstorm and observed what happened when a lightning bolt struck the kite. The lightning was conducted to the ground, behaving just like sparks made in his laboratory. Franklin showed that lightning is caused by electricity, but he mistakenly thought it was carried by a fluid.

ELECTRIFIED SOCKS

Many observations were made about the effects of electricity. People could make it, store it, and pass sparks of it between objects. In 1758 Robert Symmer (c. 1707-1763) noticed that his silk socks behaved in a strange way as he took them off. They produced sparks and would often fill out, like a wind sock in a strong wind. The socks seemed to be filled with electrical fluid that produced sparks as it passed from his leg to the socks. These effects are actually caused by static electricity (pp. 22-23), an imbalance of electrical charge between the body and the socks.

Heat energy

FORGING WITH FIRE
Fire (pp. 10-11) has been used by humans for thousands of years to provide light, warmth, and the heat needed for cooking and smelting. Forging is the art of heating metal in fire and then hammering it into shapes, such as horseshoes.

DURING THE 17TH AND 18TH CENTURIES there was disagreement about the actual nature of heat. Some people thought heat was a fluid, called "caloric," that passed from hot to cold. Others thought heat was the motion of the particles that make up matter. Joseph Black (1728-1799), a Scottish chemist who followed the caloric theory of heat, believed that "temperature" was the concentration of caloric in an object, and founded a new science called "calorimetry." But a series of experiments involving friction demonstrated that heat could be generated from muscle energy. This put an end to the caloric theory. Heat was finally shown to be a form of energy by the experiments of James Joule (pp. 24-25). Thermodynamics (pp. 26-27) – the study of heat as energy – was born. It is now known that heat is simply the kinetic energy of the countless moving atoms and molecules of matter. The hotter something is, the faster its atoms and molecules move.

This side shows Fahrenheit

This side shows Celsius

HEAT FROM CHEMICALS
When chemical reactions take place there is often a rise or fall in temperature, as heat energy is released or taken in. Some reactions need an energy input in order to take place. Others give out energy, as when water is added to calcium oxide, or quicklime. As the molecules of the two substances rearrange to form a new substance, calcium hydroxide, they release chemical potential energy (pp. 14-15) which had been stored between them. The released energy makes the atoms and molecules move more quickly, so the temperature rises.

Cold water

The calcium oxide and water are mixed together in this vessel

The alcohol inside the tube expands as its molecules move more quickly

Steam condenses on the inside of the flask

MEASURING TEMPERATURE
The temperature of any substance is directly related to the average kinetic energy (pp. 16-17) of the atoms or molecules of which it is made. Although the lowest temperature on this thermometer is -4° F (-20° C), the lowest possible temperature (called absolute zero) is about -459° F (-273° C). This temperature occurs only when atoms and molecules have no kinetic energy, or motion, at all. Fahrenheit (F) and Celsius (C) are the most commonly used scales of temperature.

Calcium oxide, also known as quicklime

Enough energy is released to boil some of the water

The lid prevents too much heat from escaping through the top

Ice is packed into these two spaces

The hot object is placed in the basket

STUDYING HEAT
Joseph Black thought that heat capacity was the amount of heat a substance could hold. It is actually a measure of how much energy is needed to raise the temperature of a substance by a particular amount. More heat is needed to raise the temperature of 2.2 lbs (1 kg) of water by 1.8° F (1° C) than to do the same to 2.2 lbs of iron, for example.

A CAPACITY FOR MELTING ICE
This is a cutaway of an "ice calorimeter" that belonged to the French scientists Antoine Lavoisier (1743-1794) and Pierre-Simon Laplace (1749-1827). With this apparatus, the amount of heat given out by a heated object as it cooled is measured. A warm object is placed in the basket, and ice is packed around it. The temperature of the ice remains at freezing as it melts with heat from the hot object. The object cools down to the same temperature as the ice, then the melted ice is let out of the calorimeter at the bottom to be weighed. This shows the capacity for heat of the object.

Melted ice runs out through this pipe

GENERATING HEAT BY FRICTION
Benjamin Thompson (1753-1814) was born in Massachusetts and was given the title Count Rumford after working for the Bavarian government. While watching the boring of cannon barrels in a Munich weapons factory, he noticed that huge amounts of heat were generated by friction between the cutting tools and the metal gun barrels. If heat were a fluid, it would have been used up very quickly, but the heat generated by friction continued to be released as long as the barrels were drilled. In the 1790s Count Rumford concluded that heat must be a form of motion.

THE LINK BETWEEN FRICTION AND HEAT
When things are rubbed, they become hot. The 19th century equipment shown here demonstrates that there is a link between mechanical "work" (kinetic energy, pp. 16-17) and heat. Water in the small copper tube heats up from the friction that occurs between the revolving copper tube and the wood as the handle is turned. The more it is turned, the hotter the water becomes – it could even be boiled.

The temperature of water in the tube can be measured with a thermometer

Handle is rapidly turned, rotating the wheel

Friction occurs when the wood and copper tube rub together

Electromagnetism

ELECTRICITY AND MAGNETISM have been known for about 3,000 years. It was noticed long ago that when some materials are rubbed, they can attract or repel other objects. Quite separately, people noticed that some natural materials seemed to have unusual powers that attracted objects with iron in them. During the 18th century, experimenters were familiar with most of the ways electricity and magnetism behave. But the two were seen as separate. Each one was thought to be carried by a "fluid" (pp. 18-19) that passed between materials, causing the attractions and repulsions people had observed. In the first half of the 19th century, an amazing discovery was made: electricity can make magnetism, and magnetism can make electricity. The discoveries of electromagnetism were very important to an understanding of energy. If these two "natural forces" could change from one to the other, maybe other "forces of nature" could do so, too. The stage was set for the development of the Law of Conservation of Energy (pp. 24-25).

MICHAEL FARADAY
One of the most important figures in the development of an understanding of electromagnetism was Englishman Michael Faraday (1791-1867). He explored the relationship between electricity and magnetism by careful and inspired experimentation at the Royal Institution in London, UK.

Magnetism

The strange, invisible forces of magnetism had puzzled people from the time magnetic rocks were discovered. What makes a compass needle move? How does a magnet know when a nearby object contains iron? Even when magnetism began to be studied in experiments, there seemed to be no connection between this "natural force" and the other "forces of nature," as they were called, such as light, gravity, heat, and electricity.

The pins are pulled to the stone by a magnetic force

LEADING THE WAY
Early people found that magnetic rocks like this would always point in the same direction if suspended on a string, making them useful to travelers for finding directions. They were named "lodestones," meaning "leading stones."

MAGNETIC COMPASS
The Earth acts as a huge magnet, for reasons which are still not fully understood. Because compasses contain magnets that are able to move freely, they respond to the Earth's magnetic field. This is an early mariners's compass. The magnet is beneath the card.

Magnetic model of the Earth

Spheres made of magnetite, a magnetic iron ore

Compass needle

Bar magnets

EXPERIMENTER'S BOX
This beautiful box from the 18th century is full of objects used to experiment with magnetism. It shows that people were fascinated by the effects of magnetism and tried to find out more about them. The first person to describe fully the various effects of magnetism was Dr. William Gilbert (1544-1603) in his book *De Magnete*. He also tried to explain the attraction of the planets to the Sun in terms of magnetism.

Electricity

Although electricity was known to the ancient Greeks, the scientific study of electricity was only really begun in the 16th century by William Gilbert. He discovered, for example, that objects "charged" with electricity either attracted (pulled) or repelled (pushed away) other "charged" objects. Electricity was studied with great interest. Many theories were put forward to explain it and how it caused objects to move and even made sparks (pp. 18-19). Scientists soon began to search for a connection between these effects and other "forces of nature."

Each coil has a total length of about 70 ft (21 m) and is wound in layers, each separated from the next by cotton cloth

AMBER ATTRACTION
Electricity seems to have been discovered in ancient Greece, probably when someone rubbed a piece of amber and noticed that it picked up light objects such as feathers. The word "electricity" is from the Greek word for amber, *elektron*. Many other things can be given static, or stationary, electricity by rubbing them. Static electricity has "potential energy" (pp. 14-15).

ELECTRICITY AND MAGNETISM
This iron ring with two coils wound around it is a replica of one used by Michael Faraday in 1831, in one of his most famous experiments. Faraday discovered that although the coils were not actually connected to each other, electricity was produced in one coil every time the electric current through the other one changed. Hans Christian Oersted had already discovered that an electric current (moving electricity) produced a magnetic effect around it (see below). Faraday realized that the "induction" of electricity in the second coil could be explained only by the presence of such a magnetic effect in the iron core. Experiments of this type paved the way for an understanding of energy. Electricity and magnetism had always been two separate things, but now it was becoming clear that they could be converted, one to the other.

TORSION BALANCE
This piece of equipment was developed by Charles Augustin de Coulomb (1738-1806) to investigate the forces between electrical charges. The metal bar in the middle is hung on a long, thin metal wire that twists if the bar turns. Static electricity was introduced into the apparatus at the two brass knobs outside the glass. The two metal spheres inside the glass also became charged (because the parts inside the glass were made of metal, through which electricity can easily pass), and attracted or repelled each other, according to the type and amount of charge introduced. Coulomb worked out the size of the forces involved from the amount the bar twisted as the spheres were pulled and pushed.

Charged objects were brought near this knob

Long, thin metal wire

Charged objects, such as amber, were brought near this knob

This sphere is fixed

Coils of copper wire

The bar is free to turn

When wires are connected to the two terminals, electricity is released

The jar contained a chemical called ammonium chloride

Wires from a battery connect to both terminals

Compass needle is magnetic

When the current flows, the needle is at right angles to the apparatus, but when there is no current, the needle points north

OERSTED'S NEEDLE
This apparatus demonstrates a discovery made in 1820 by Hans Christian Oersted (1777-1851). When an electric current flowed above and below the compass needle, the needle swung across the wire. This seemed to show that the current was producing a magnetic effect. Energy in the form of electric current changes into magnetic energy, which makes the magnetic needle move.

The scale shows how much the bar turns

EARLY BATTERY
The Leclanché cell is an early example of what is commonly called a battery. The cell provided a supply of current, or moving, electricity, which could be used by scientists in their experiments. Most batteries used today are actually Leclanché cells, tightly cased in metal rather than a glass jar.

The porous pot contained a mixture of carbon and manganese dioxide

The conservation of energy

BY THE 1840S IT HAD BECOME APPARENT that the "forces of nature," which had been thought of as separate "imponderable fluids" (pp. 18-19), could be transformed into each other. For example, the work of Oersted and Faraday (pp. 22-23) showed that electricity and magnetism can change from one to the other. Mechanical "work," such as lifting a weight, can be converted to heat by friction (pp. 20-21). It was the painstaking work of the amateur scientist James Joule (1818-1889) that began to prove that "energy," as it became known, can not be created or destroyed, it can only change in form. This idea is known as the conservation of energy.

NATURAL FORCES
In 1847, German scientist Hermann von Helmholtz (1821-1894) became the first person to explain the conservation of energy clearly. He said that all natural forces are either "living" (kinetic energy, pp. 16-17) or "tensional" (potential energy, pp. 14-15) and can be converted into one another. The word energy did not take on its current scientific meaning until the mid-19th century.

As the handle is turned, the small electromagnet spins

The whole box is placed in the middle of a huge electromagnet

Gearing transfers kinetic energy from handle to electromagnet

JAMES PRESCOTT JOULE
The son of a wealthy English brewer, Joule converted a room in his father's house into a laboratory. In 1838 he began his measurements of heat given out by various processes. He even spent much of his honeymoon studying a waterfall, trying to show that heat was produced as the water splashed into the pool at the bottom. The unit of energy, the joule (pp. 36-37), was named after him.

JOULE'S REVOLVING ELECTROMAGNET
In the early part of the 1840s Joule wanted to show that the electrical energy generated by mechanical energy in a dynamo can produce another form of energy, heat. He built a small revolving electromagnet, which was turned rapidly between the poles of another electromagnet that surrounded the box shown here. He enclosed the revolving electromagnet in a glass tube full of water and measured the temperature of the water before and after the experiment to within $\frac{1}{30}$ of a degree Fahrenheit ($\frac{1}{50}$ Celsius). As the electromagnet spun it generated an electric current that could be measured by a sensitive meter. Joule found that the current warmed the water. The amount of heat produced was always directly related to the electric current, which was in turn directly related to the amount of mechanical work used to turn the handle.

HEATING BY STIRRING

Joule knew that the heat produced in his revolving electromagnet came from the muscle energy that was used to turn its handle. So he wanted to find the relationship between this mechanical "work" and heat. Joule's most famous experiment, in which no electric current was involved, did just that. The apparatus consisted of a brass paddlewheel that stirred water in a copper vessel. The paddlewheel was turned by falling weights. As the weights fell, they possessed mechanical, or kinetic (pp. 16-17), energy. Joule let the weights fall many times. The weights turned the paddlewheel and stirred the water as they fell. Each time the temperature of the water rose by an amount that depended on how far the weights fell. This showed that the kinetic energy of the weights as they fell now existed as heat energy in the water.

Handle allows the weights to be lifted

Ropes are attached over pulleys to weights

A very sensitive thermometer is placed in this hole

Vanes break up the flow of the water in the vessel

Copper vessel holds water

Metal spindle is oiled to reduce heat energy loss through friction

A paddle inside the vessel is turned by these pulley wheels

Pulley wheels of different sizes allow the paddle to be turned at different speeds

Water is held in this vessel

The amount of heat energy absorbed by the apparatus can be taken into account, making the experiment very accurate

Iron bound by ribbon of oiled silk

Glass cylinder is filled with water and corked during the experiment

The electromagnet's core is made of six strips of iron, separated by oiled paper

Foil with slit interrupts electromagnetic currents

Wooden sticks are wrapped in varnished flannel to produce a layer of air in the apparatus

Silk-covered copper wire is wrapped around the iron core

Wires to meter

Wire dips into mercury to make a connection to a meter

THE MECHANICAL EQUIVALENT OF HEAT

This apparatus, made in 1884, is similar to Joule's paddle-wheel apparatus, but it gave a more accurate figure for the "mechanical equivalent of heat." The amount of heat energy needed to raise the temperature of 2.2 lb (1 kg) of water by 1.8° F (1° C) is one kilocalorie, or about 4,000 joules. This is the same amount of mechanical energy needed to lift a 4-ton weight by 4 inches (10 cm).

Muscles use chemical energy from food to produce mechanical energy

Light passes through pinhole

Chemicals on photographic plate record light

Bulb converts electricity to light

Dynamo produces electricity for bulb

CONVERTING FORMS OF ENERGY

Joule's experiments proved that when one form of energy is converted into another, no energy is destroyed. For example, food (a source of chemical potential energy) is used to make muscles work. The muscle energy is used to turn the handle of a dynamo, and this energy is converted to electrical energy. This electrical energy is then converted into the heat and light produced by a light bulb, and next some of the light energy is captured on a photographic plate. Thus, some of the original chemical potential energy becomes chemical potential energy again. The total amount of energy in this scenario remains the same – it is the amount that was provided at the outset by the chemical potential energy from the food.

Thermodynamics

Heat behaves in a predictable way. For example, when ice is placed in hot water, it melts. Heat – and other forms of energy – acts as if it obeys "laws" that restrict its behavior, and the study of heat as a form of energy is called thermodynamics. The "laws of thermodynamics" were worked out during the mid 19th century. The "law of conservation of energy" (pp. 24-25) says that energy cannot be created or destroyed, but can only change from one form to another. This is the first law of thermodynamics. Any form of energy can be converted entirely into heat. But when heat energy is changed into other forms, it can never do so entirely. Some of it always remains as heat, and temperatures always even out. This is the second law of thermodynamics. The behavior of heat energy can be explained by the fact that it is the motion of particles of matter – atoms and molecules. The temperature of matter is the average energy of all its particles. Conduction, the transfer of heat between matter in contact, happens because the particles of a hot object transfer some of their energy to those of a cooler object.

COOL BOTTLE
This bottle from the Sudan was designed to keep drinks cold on hot days. To work, the bottle itself must be wet. Water on the side of the bottle evaporates, and this requires energy. The energy is supplied by the bottle and its contents in the form of heat. As they lose heat, they become cooler. This is what happens to a person when they are wet on a hot day and is why they feel cold.

FOREVER IN MOTION
No machine can ever be 100 percent efficient because a certain amount of energy will always be lost as heat. This means that there can be no such thing as a perpetual motion machine, which would work forever and never run out of energy, but many people still try to make one. This attempt was built in 1747. Iron balls fell on to a large wheel and turned the wheel around to operate the diagonal screw. The screw would then lift the balls up to repeat the process perpetually. But in practice the machine did not work because it would eventually slow down to a halt as its energy was lost as heat.

Liquid is put into flask through top opening

Top of the flask is closed to prevent convection

STOPPING THE ESCAPE OF HEAT
The vacuum flask, or Dewar flask, was invented by the Scottish physicist James Dewar (1842-1923). This is one of Dewar's experimental flasks that has been cut away to reveal the inside. The flask contains a partial vacuum between its walls that greatly reduces conduction, the transfer of heat energy between matter in contact. A perfect vacuum contains no matter, so it does not conduct heat. Heat energy can become radiation (pp. 40-41) and can pass between particles, even in a vacuum, but the vacuum flask has silvered walls that reflect radiated heat. The flask is closed to maintain the vacuum and prevent convection, the transfer of heat by air circulation.

Air is taken out through this tube to create a vacuum

Vacuum between the inner and outer walls prevents conduction

Liquid is kept inside

Silvered walls reflect radiated heat

AN INTELLIGENT BOTTLE?
A variation of the vacuum flask invented by Dewar (above right) was mass-produced in the early 20th century and sold under the trade name Thermos. Because they keep hot drinks hot and cold drinks cold, they are useful for picnics, as this 1940s advertisement shows. The flasks cannot tell the difference between temperatures, but their internal vacuum stops conduction, so the temperature of the liquid does not change.

Water pipe

Thermometers measure the temperature of the cooling water

Air is pumped in here

Dial gives measurement of pressure

Insulation prevents heat from outside warming the liquid gas

Pipe brings cold air back to the top

Water circulates here

Liquid collects here

Liquid is drained off here

Pressurized air is forced through nozzle

HOW TO MAKE AIR LIQUID

Air is a mixture of gases. If gases are cooled enough, they become liquids. One way of doing this is by forcing them to expand suddenly. This is what happens in a Hampson Air Liquifier. Air is pumped in at the top under pressure. It is forced through the tiny nozzle at the bottom, and as it leaves the nozzle it expands into an almost empty space. This expansion requires energy, which has to come from within the gas, so the gas cools. The cooling effect is large enough to make some of the air change to a liquid form. The rest of the air is pumped around again to repeat the process.

Pipes carry water to cool the pressurized gas, which heats up as it is pressurized

The glass cover prevents breezes from turning the vanes

Vanes turn when electromagnetic radiation falls on them

One side of each aluminum vane is coated with mica, which absorbs more of the radiation

Gas molecules travel at many hundreds of mph (km/h)

TURNING THE VANES

There are millions and millions of air molecules inside the glass cover of this Crookes's radiometer. They are all moving around randomly, bouncing into each other, the vanes, and the glass. One side of each vane gets hotter than the other side because it is coated with mica, which absorbs more electromagnetic radiation (pp. 40-41), such as light, than aluminum, which is reflective. This warms the surrounding air, which further increases the speed of the molecules. They bump into the vane more often on the warm side, pushing it around.

FREEZING HOT

When ice is placed into a hot liquid, the ice will melt and become liquid, and the liquid will cool. But why does the liquid not solidify to become ice? Because heat energy passes from hot to cold, eventually evening out. This is the second law of thermodynamics. As the ice cubes in the glass melt with the heat energy from the hot water, the water cools. This will continue until the mixture is at the same temperature throughout. It is possible to make heat energy pass from cold objects to hot, but to do so energy needs to be supplied; for example, in a refrigerator, where it is supplied by the energy used in running the refrigeration process.

PARTICLES OF ICE AND LIQUID

Thinking of matter in terms of its particles helps to explain why ice cubes melt in hot water. The water molecules that make up an ice cube have less kinetic energy (pp. 16-17) than those of the hot water, and merely vibrate around a fixed position. Hot water molecules have more kinetic energy and move around randomly. Sometimes they bump into molecules at the edge of the ice cube and transfer some of their kinetic energy to them. This transfer of kinetic energy then continues until the energy is shared between all the molecules in the mixture. The molecules in the ice are given enough kinetic energy to break free of each other, and they become liquid water. The hot water molecules slow down as they lose some of their energy, which means that they will become cooler. Eventually, the whole mixture will become the same temperature.

Ice cube   Hot water   Hot water molecules move randomly, bumping into each other

Ice molecules have too little energy to break free

Steam energy

WHEN STEAM CONDENSES, or turns back into water, it suddenly occupies a much smaller space than before. If a piston is put between the condensing steam and the air, it will be moved as the air pushes down to fill the space. By connecting the piston to a pump, the energy of the air can be used to pump water from flooded mines. Before the steam engine, flooding in coal mines had been tackled using pumps driven by animals or water wheels (pp. 12-13). The first practical steam engine was put into operation in 1712 by English inventor Thomas Newcomen (1663-1729). His engines were very successful, but the design was greatly improved by James Watt of Scotland. Watt made the steam engine more efficient and designed it to produce circular motion, which could drive many machines other than pumps.

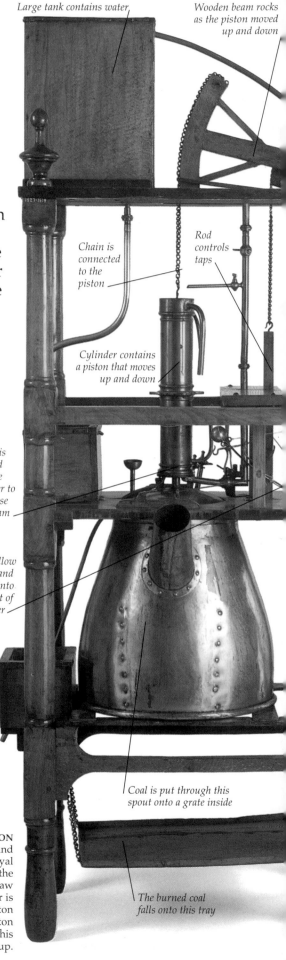

Large tank contains water

Wooden beam rocks as the piston moved up and down

Chain is connected to the piston

Rod controls taps

Cylinder contains a piston that moves up and down

Water is sprayed into the cylinder to condense the steam

Taps allow steam and water into and out of cylinder

Coal is put through this spout onto a grate inside

The burned coal falls onto this tray

MINERS FRIEND
Thomas Savery (1650-1715) patented the design for this steam pump in 1698. The pump was intended to clear water from flooded mines, but the pipes carrying the steam often burst.

As the steam excapes here, the ball rotates

The steam is forced through the pipes and into the ball

Water is placed in the boiler and heated

A fire provides the heat energy to boil water in the boiler

HERO'S AEOLIPILE
This is a model of an aeolipile, invented by a Greek engineer, Hero of Alexandria (c. AD 100). It was a forerunner of Parsons's steam turbine (pp. 32-33). Water in the boiler gained heat energy from a fire underneath. As the water boiled, steam was formed and forced out through the holes in the arms of the ball. The ball turned as a "reaction" to the escape of steam, so this is a "reaction turbine." The machine was not powerful enough to do any useful work.

EXPERIMENTS WITH STEAM
Willem s'Gravesande (pp. 16-17) used this small copper sphere in his experiments with gases. The sphere contained water, which was heated to boiling point over a fire. The sphere was then fixed to the wheels, and a hole in the sphere was opened. The force of the escaping steam pushed the sphere forward.

A ROYAL DEMONSTRATION
This small steam engine was made by or for John Theophilus Desaguliers (1683-1744) around 1740 to demonstrate the principles of the "atmospheric" steam engine to the British royal family. An atmospheric engine creates a near vacuum, usually beneath a piston, so that the air pressure on the other side can push the piston. This is the same way that a drinking straw works, except that instead of sucking air out to create the vacuum, steam from a boiler is "condensed" to form water in a cylinder, leaving mostly empty space. The air above the piston pushes with the force of atmospheric pressure. The energy is actually transferred to the piston from the millions of air molecules that hit the top of the piston each second (pp. 26-27). This model used steam energy to pump water from a bucket on the floor to the box halfway up.

SPRAYING COLD WATER

Thomas Newcomen's steam engine (see right) was an atmospheric engine that pumped water from the bottom of a mine at the rate of 440 gal (2,000 L) per minute. The steam condensed inside the cylinder when cold water was sprayed into it. This was inefficient, because heat was wasted as the cylinder cooled. James Watt improved this by making the steam condense away from the cylinder, so the cylinder was kept hot.

Motion of beam pulls piston up

Cylinder

Beam tilts back and forth

Weight pulls down on the beam

Pump rod

Cold water condenses steam

Piston pushed down by the air above

Boiler

Fire

Weight

Pump lifts water

Water is released from the mine

1 THE PISTON RISES
Atmospheric steam engines work on a simple principle. First, the weight of the pump rod pulls down on the beam, lifting the piston. This fills the cylinder with steam from the boiler.

2 THE PISTON FALLS
Cold water is sprayed into the cylinder. The steam loses heat energy, changing back into water. The air above the piston now pushes it down. The beam tilts and works the pump.

Water is pulled up from the bucket and flows out of this tap

Chain is connected to the rods of the pumps

The rods of the pump are heavy and pull the piston back up the cylinder

STEAM IN THE FACTORY
The steam engine had a huge impact on industry. Once engines could produce circular motion, they could take over from water wheels (pp. 12-13) to provide energy in factories. Factories could then run more powerful machines, and they no longer needed to be built by a river. The steam engine in this cotton mill was in another room, and its energy was transmitted to the machinery by pulleys and belts.

Exhaust escapes from this pipe

Exhaust gases from the boiler go past the cylinder and the boiler, helping to keep them hot

Coal goes into hatch

Cylinder stays hot inside the boiler, so wastes less energy

Crank is connected to the piston, and turns the wheels of the steam engine

Handle for the driver

Water is taken up from a bucket that is placed at the bottom of this pipe

HIGH-PRESSURE STEAM
Until 1800, all steam engines were atmospheric engines, because the boilers could not withstand steam at pressures much higher than that of the atmosphere. The first person to use high-pressure steam was Englishman Richard Trevithick (1771-1833), who built the first locomotive in 1804. Similar work was done in the US by Oliver Evans (1755-1819). High-pressure engines, like this Trevithick locomotive, used more coal and were more powerful than atmospheric engines. This allowed steam to be used for transport (pp. 30-31).

Richard Trevithick

Footplate for the driver

Boiler is made from 1½-in (38-mm) thick metal

Model of Trevithick's London locomotive, *Catch Me Who Can*

Energy for transport

MOVING PEOPLE AND GOODS from place to place is a vital part of any civilization. The earliest ways of getting around made use of animals (pp. 8-9) and wind (pp. 12-13) as energy sources. Toward the end of the 18th century, the first canals were built – with horses providing the energy to drag barges along canals. But everyday travel on land was still slow and awkward. At the beginning of the 19th century, the steam engine (pp. 28-29) became powerful enough to be given wheels and take its energy source of coal with it. The railway age had begun, and soon trains were carrying passengers and freight in many countries. By the end of the 19th century, the internal combustion engine had been invented. It made use of the energy released by rapidly burning fuel inside its cylinders, making motor vehicles possible. As technology improved in the 20th century, other forms of transportation appeared, such as streetcars and aircraft.

ONE HORSEPOWER
The horse has always been an important source of energy for transportation. Assyrian horse-drawn chariots like this were very fast and used in races and for hunting. Groups of horses were used for transport in many other ways. Stagecoaches often used 12 horses to pull them. In 1783 James Watt defined the power of one horse as a unit of power, the "horsepower."

Steering wheel

Horizontal cylinder

Passenger seat

Driver's seat

Oak frame

Brake

The engine ran on gasoline

Belts transmit energy to the wheels

ENERGY CARRIAGE
The internal combustion engine is compact and powerful enough for its energy source – usually gasoline – to be carried with it. This is a model of a motor carriage made in 1875 by Siegfried Marcus, an Austrian engineer. The car had a top speed of about 4 mph (6 km/h). Although it worked remarkably well for its time, Marcus did not realize the potential of his motor car. It was another 11 years before the first real motor car appeared on the market. It was made by Karl Benz (1844-1929) of Germany.

FOUR-CYLINDER ENGINE
This engine from a 1920s Austin Seven motor car is cut away to show inside one of the cylinders. The engine has four cylinders, each containing a piston that moves up and down about 2,400 times per minute. The piston's motion can be described by four movements, or strokes. First, the piston moves down, and gasoline vapor is sucked into the cylinder from the carburetor. Then, the piston moves up again to compress the vapor at the top of the cylinder. This is the "compression stroke." Next, a spark from the spark plug causes the gasoline vapor to explode, forcing the piston down the cylinder again. This supplies the energy for the car. Finally, the piston moves back up, pushing the used fuel out to the exhaust pipe. This "four-stroke cycle" has been used in most motor vehicles made since 1876.

MOVING STEAM ENGINES
Locomotives took over from stagecoaches and canals when people began to realize that they were faster and more powerful. The first passenger railroad opened in 1830 in the UK. There was much opposition to the railroads, mainly from the owners of canals and stagecoach companies. Many people were afraid of the railroads because they thought it was dangerous to travel at speeds greater than 12 mph (20 km/h).

OTTO'S ENGINE
In 1876 Nikolaus Otto of Germany became the first person to build and sell a four-stroke engine – on which most later engines have been based. He called it the "Silent Otto" because it ran so quietly. One of the main features of the four-stroke engine is the "compression stroke." More energy is released if the fuel is a vapor under pressure. The idea was first developed by a Frenchman, Alphonse Beau de Rochas (1815-1891), but it was Otto who made it a success.

Pulley wheel is connected to the dynamo

Camshaft sprocket connects crankshaft to camshaft

INNOVATIVE DEVELOPMENTS IN CITY TRANSPORT

This is a model of a streetcar that was part of a transport service run in London, UK, in the early 1900s. The first streetcars appeared in New York City in 1832. They were horse-drawn, but soon other energy sources were tried – first steam, then electricity. The first electric streetcars were introduced in Berlin, Germany, in 1881. They used electric rails in the road, which could be dangerous. As an alternative, overhead cables were developed. Electricity with high potential energy (pp. 14-15) was supplied through the wires, powering an electric motor in the car that turned the wheels. Streetcars, like trains, must stay on rails. In a crowded city street this could be a problem, so streetcars were soon replaced in most places by other forms of transportation, such as buses. However, streetcars can help prevent traffic jams and are appearing in some cities again. Streetcars have the added advantage of being less polluting than other forms of transport.

Upper passenger deck

These pantographs collect electricity from overhead wires

Handle controls the speed of the streetcar

Exhaust valve allows the exhaust out of the cylinder

Piston (cutaway)

Inlet valve allows gasoline vapor and air to enter the cylinder

Cylinder (cutaway)

Spark plug

Inlet manifold takes gasoline and air into engine

L.C.C.

Lower passenger deck

The driver can operate the streetcar from either end, so that it does not have to turn around

Carburetor, where liquid gasoline is vaporized and mixed with air

Flywheel keeps the crankshaft turning

The camshaft controls the valve as it turns

Connecting rod links piston to crankshaft

Crankshaft is driven by pistons

Crankcase

Sump is reservoir for oil, which reduces friction

ENERGY FOR FLIGHT

Getting into the air and staying up takes a lot of energy. Before planes were invented, some people tried to fly by attaching wings to themselves and flapping them. These efforts failed because, unlike birds, humans do not have muscles powerful enough to keep them in the air. Although steam-powered machines were suggested, none of them would have worked, because steam engines do not produce enough power to lift their own weight. The internal combustion engine is more powerful and efficient for its weight and was used by the Wright Brothers for the first powered flight in 1903. The jet engine is more powerful still, producing enough power to keep a large airliner in the air. The NASA Space Shuttle burns fuel in a large rocket to provide the energy it needs to escape the Earth's gravity. Large amounts of the fuel's energy are wasted, and a bright light and intense heat accompany the Shuttle's take-off.

Generating electricity

ELECTRICITY IS THE MOST CONVENIENT form of energy to use in the home and in many parts of industry. But electricity must be produced, or generated. There are many ways to generate a voltage, or electrical potential energy (pp. 14-15), but the best way is to use electromagnetism (pp. 22-23). Michael Faraday visualized a magnet's energy as a "field." When metal moves through a "magnetic field," a voltage is produced. Using this effect, various "magnetoelectric" machines were developed, and by the end of the 19th century steam engines (pp. 28-29) and water turbines (p. 58) were turning large generators to make electricity for homes, offices, and factories. One very important invention that enabled electricity to be generated on a large scale was the steam turbine. It was much faster and more efficient than the steam engines that had been used before. Steam turbines are still used to drive most generators.

GRAMME DYNAMO

A dynamo is a machine that turns mechanical energy (p. 8–9) into electrical energy. Zénobe Théophile Gramme (1826-1901) of Belgium invented the first practical dynamo in 1870. This one produced "direct current," or DC. Direct-current electricity cannot be distributed over large distances, so this dynamo supplied electricity only on a small scale. The coils in the middle of the dynamo were turned at high speed by a steam engine, and the two large coils produced a magnetic field around them. This generated the electricity.

STEAM TURBINE GENERATOR

Until the invention of the steam turbine in 1884, dynamos and generators were powered by traditional steam engines. But these were inefficient and could not turn fast enough to produce electricity on a large scale. The steam turbine was developed by the Irish engineer Sir Charles Parsons (1854-1931). The steam turbine here made use of the energy of high-pressure steam at 400° F (200° C) to drive the generator. The turbine turned 4,800 times every minute, and yet it ran so smoothly that it did not have to be bolted down. It generated 100,000 joules (pp. 36-37) of electrical energy every second (100 kW).

Sir Charles Parsons

Wires through which electricity leaves the generator

The governor keeps the machine turning at the correct speed

The generator

Powerful magnets turn inside these coils

Parsons's steam turbine, built in 1889

EARLY POWER STATION

By 1882, American inventor Thomas Edison was operating a power plant in New York City. The use of electricity soon spread to much of the world. This is a model of a power station built at Deptford, in London, UK. It began generating electricity in 1889, and it was capable of supplying electrical energy at a rate of over one million joules every second. It was designed by Sebastian Ziani de Ferranti (1864-1930), an engineer living in London. It was the largest and most powerful power station of its time and provided energy for half of London. It was powered by a huge steam engine. All large power stations since the beginning of the 20th century have run on either steam turbines or water turbines. As electricity came to be supplied on a large scale, its energy could be used in an ever-increasing number of ways, in industry and in the home (pp. 34-35).

Steam is allowed in here to slow the turbine when excess electricity is generated

This lever is held down to start the turbine

Steam inlet

Valve controled by governor

Huge "triple-expansion" steam engines made the most of the energy of steam by letting it expand in three stages

Turbine blades

The steam to drive the engines was produced by burning coal in boilers in another part of the station

Electric lighting

Notice how small a person is, compared to the generators

This wheel rotates rapidly to prevent the valve from seizing up

HOW THE STEAM TURBINE WORKS

Steam entered at the top of Parsons's steam turbine and forced its way down, past the valve. It found its way into the axle of the turbine blades and then pushed its way out, turning the blades as it did so. As the steam finished in one blade, it went to the next. Each blade is slightly bigger than the next – this is because to get the energy from the steam, the steam must be allowed to expand. For the same reason, the steam outlet is bigger than the steam inlet.

Steam inlet

Inside the turbine are rows of turbine blades

Steam outlet

Tray catches drips of oil

PYLONS AND TRANSFORMERS

To distribute electrical energy over large distances, it is transformed, or changed, to a high voltage (usually between 132,000 and 400,000 volts) before being transformed back to smaller voltages (between 110 and 240 volts). There are transformers at each end of the line – at the power station and at local "substations." Alternating current is used because direct current cannot be transformed and does not travel well. The system for distributing electricity was devised by an Eastern European-born American electrical engineer, Nikola Tesla (1856-1943). Pylons carrying overhead cables are the most common way of distributing electricity, because digging power lines underground can be expensive. The large cooling towers are a familiar sight at power stations. They cool the water that is used to condense the steam that leaves the turbines, turning the steam back into water.

Energy in the home

For thousands of years people have used energy to cook their food and to provide heat and light in their homes. This energy was usually obtained from fire (pp. 10-11) by burning wood, oil, or candles. During the 19th century, coal gas (pp. 54-55) began to be used in millions of homes in many countries. Later, powerful electrical generators (pp. 32-33) were built to supply electricity to homes. Electricity is more convenient than gas as a source of energy in the home because it can be used for jobs other than heating, lighting, and cooking. It provides the energy for an ever-increasing variety of appliances such as hair driers, microwave ovens, and televisions.

Glass chimney

Etched glass shade makes the light from the lamp more diffuse, or spread out

THE WARM GLOW OF KEROSENE
Kerosene is a part of the mixture that makes up crude oil, but it can also be made from coal or wood. Kerosene lamps have a wick that slowly absorbs the fuel, and the amount of light given out can be controlled by lowering or raising the wick. The wick burns away by only a small amount. With heat, the kerosene turns into a vapor and burns strongly around the wick. The burning vapor gives out intense light because it is so hot. Kerosene lamps such as this were used a great deal during the late 19th century because they gave good, controllable light. The glass chimney was an important invention, because it increased the draft around the wick, making the flame burn more brightly.

Knob to raise or lower wick

Holes allow fresh air to the wick

Kerosene burns with a smokeless flame

Fuel is kept in this container

FIREWOOD FOR THE WINTER
The people in this medieval picture are using energy from fire to help them cook and keep warm in the winter. Outside the cottage, people are chopping and gathering firewood. As the wood burns, it releases heat and light. The glow of the flames can just be seen, and a woman and baby are sitting in front of the hearth to keep warm.

COOKING WITH SPIRITS
Denatured alcohol, or spirits, was used as a fuel in this portable stove invented in 1850. The fuel was held in the closed container above the cage, which held a wick. When the wick was lit, it heated the fuel above it. The heat vaporized the fuel, which escaped under pressure through the nozzle. As it escaped, the fuel was ignited by the second wick, and this produced a flame that roared into the chamber, above which a pot or pan of food was placed.

Cooking pot is placed on ring

Flame roars through opening

Fuel escapes through nozzle, which faces second wick when in use

Kerosene is kept in brass tank reservoir

Second wick ignites vaporized fuel

Wick is lit to heat fuel

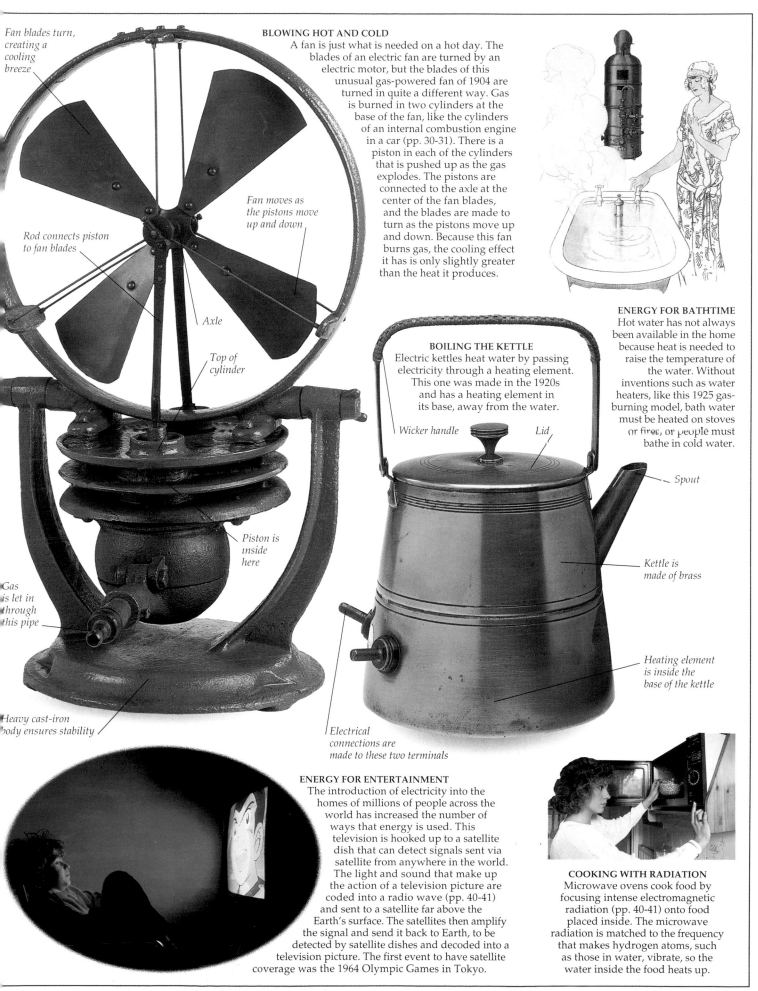

Fan blades turn, creating a cooling breeze

BLOWING HOT AND COLD

A fan is just what is needed on a hot day. The blades of an electric fan are turned by an electric motor, but the blades of this unusual gas-powered fan of 1904 are turned in quite a different way. Gas is burned in two cylinders at the base of the fan, like the cylinders of an internal combustion engine in a car (pp. 30-31). There is a piston in each of the cylinders that is pushed up as the gas explodes. The pistons are connected to the axle at the center of the fan blades, and the blades are made to turn as the pistons move up and down. Because this fan burns gas, the cooling effect it has is only slightly greater than the heat it produces.

Fan moves as the pistons move up and down

Rod connects piston to fan blades

Axle

Top of cylinder

Piston is inside here

Gas is let in through this pipe

Heavy cast-iron body ensures stability

BOILING THE KETTLE

Electric kettles heat water by passing electricity through a heating element. This one was made in the 1920s and has a heating element in its base, away from the water.

Wicker handle

Lid

ENERGY FOR BATHTIME

Hot water has not always been available in the home because heat is needed to raise the temperature of the water. Without inventions such as water heaters, like this 1925 gas-burning model, bath water must be heated on stoves or fires, or people must bathe in cold water.

Spout

Kettle is made of brass

Heating element is inside the base of the kettle

Electrical connections are made to these two terminals

ENERGY FOR ENTERTAINMENT

The introduction of electricity into the homes of millions of people across the world has increased the number of ways that energy is used. This television is hooked up to a satellite dish that can detect signals sent via satellite from anywhere in the world. The light and sound that make up the action of a television picture are coded into a radio wave (pp. 40-41) and sent to a satellite far above the Earth's surface. The satellites then amplify the signal and send it back to Earth, to be detected by satellite dishes and decoded into a television picture. The first event to have satellite coverage was the 1964 Olympic Games in Tokyo.

COOKING WITH RADIATION

Microwave ovens cook food by focusing intense electromagnetic radiation (pp. 40-41) onto food placed inside. The microwave radiation is matched to the frequency that makes hydrogen atoms, such as those in water, vibrate, so the water inside the food heats up.

Measuring energy

THERE ARE MANY SITUATIONS in which there is a need to know how much energy is being changed from one form to another. For example, a company that generates electricity needs a way to find out how much electrical energy is used by each of its customers. In most scientific experiments there is some form of energy measurement. A meter is an instrument that measures energy, and the standard unit of energy is the joule (J), named after James Joule (pp. 24-25). But energy can be measured in many different units. A Calorie (pp. 52-53) is defined as the amount of heat energy (pp. 20-21) needed to raise the temperature of 2.2 lb (1 kg) of water by 1.8°F (1°C). Power is simply the rate at which the energy is changed. The watt (W) is the unit of power and is named after James Watt (pp. 28-29).

One W means 1 J of energy being changed each second. So, a 1,000 W (1 kW) electrical appliance changes 1,000 J (1 kJ) of electrical energy into the same amount of heat energy each second. If the appliance was left on for one hour, it would use 3,600 kJ, or 1 kilowatt-hour (1 kWh) of electrical energy.

NATURAL ENERGY METERS
Human and animal brains receive signals from specialized nerve endings, which measure energy, or changes in energy. This picture shows the light-sensitive receptors of the eye, which measure the light energy that enters the eye. There are nerves that are sensitive to heat and pressure in the skin, to light in the eyes, and to vibrations in the ears. Without these energy sensors, humans and animals would have no way of sensing the world around them.

MOVING NEEDLE METER
Electricity is the most commonly used form of energy, and there are many ways of measuring it. When working with electric circuits, it is usually important to know how much electricity is being supplied (current), and how much energy each unit of electricity is able to supply (voltage). Most meters to measure electricity work by changing a little of the electrical energy into magnetism, and making the resulting magnetic force move a needle on a dial. This meter from the late 1800s was one of the first to measure current and voltage reliably.

Cutaway of electric current meter, or ammeter (side view)

Top view of an electric current meter, or ammeter

Coil produces a magnetic force which depends on the current flowing

Wires can be connected to these terminals

Electricity passes through these coils and produces magnetism

Small magnet is turned by the magnetism from the coils, causing the needle to move

Glass protects the needle from damage and from air currents, which can affect the measurement

Wires are connected to these terminals to complete the circuit

Moveable weight

ELECTRICAL SCALES
This "steelyard ammeter," made in the late 19th century, measured the current of electricity flowing in laboratory experiments. The more current, the farther along the scale the weight had to be moved to balance the magnetic force produced in the coil. The current is a measure of its rate of flow. The voltage of electricity is a measure of its energy. The total power, or amount of electrical energy supplied every second, is simply equal to the current multiplied by the voltage. Large power stations can supply electrical energy at a rate of thousands of millions of joules each second.

Scale

BURNING FUEL
Different fuels can release different amounts of chemical energy as heat. This is denatured alcohol, which is often used as a fuel for small stoves (pp. 34-35). Denatured alcohol, butane, propane, and paraffin are all common domestic fuels. Gasoline, another common fuel, is used mainly in car engines (pp. 30-31). 1.76 pints (1 l) of gasoline will release about 40 million J when burned completely. Depending on how it is burned, most of this will become heat immediately. This makes it a very convenient fuel to burn in engines.

ONE JOULE OF ENERGY
The international unit of energy is the joule. An apple weighing about 3.5 oz (100 g) lifted 39 in (1 m) is given 1 joule (1 J) of potential energy (pp. 14-15). If it is dropped through the same distance, that 1 J of potential energy will be changed to 1 J of kinetic energy (pp. 16-17) as it falls, and then to 1 J of heat and sound energy as it hits the ground. A 60-W light bulb changes 60 J of electrical energy into light and heat every second. That is enough energy to lift 60 apples 39 in (1 m). The Sun (pp. 48-49) radiates 39,000 million million J of energy into space every second.

THERMAL ENERGY
The molecules of any substance are in constant motion, so they possess kinetic energy (pp. 16-17). The temperature of a substance is related to the average kinetic energy of all of the particles of which it is made. A thermometer is an energy measuring device. The jam in this jar is at a temperature of 152°F (67°C). Each of the molecules of the jam has a tiny amount of kinetic energy. There are so many molecules that the total heat energy, or thermal energy, of the jam is about 58,000 J.

DRIVING A CAR
All the energy that a car uses to accelerate and keep moving comes from the gasoline or diesel fuel it burns in its engine. A typical "fuel-efficient" car will use about 1.3 gal (6 l) of fuel on a 60-mile (100-km) journey. This means that about 240 million J of energy is obtained from the fuel. Only about one-third of the energy obtained from the fuel turns the wheels. Some cars can produce 100 "horsepower." One horsepower is about 746 W (746 J/sec), which is approximately the power that a horse can develop in pulling a load.

A MESSAGE IN SMOKE

Before the invention of the telegraph, long-distance communication was very difficult. Smoke signals were one way to get a message beyond shouting distance, but they were useful for communicating only in clear daylight. They were used in many parts of the world, including China, Australia, and North America. At night, when smoke signals could not be seen, the light of fires was used to send messages. There were many other methods of long-distance communication that did not rely on electricity, such as beating logs and drums, or signaling with flags.

Energy for communication

ALL FORMS OF COMMUNICATION require energy – both to create a message and to send it. A person waving to another, for example, needs energy for moving his or her hand, then light energy transmits the image of the wave to the other person. Because of this need for energy, communicating over large distances was difficult before the use of electricity, which made communication much faster and easier. The first large-scale form of communication to use electricity was the telegraph. One of the first successful telegraphs was constructed in 1837. It consisted of compass needles that turned as a current flowed through a wire. Over the next century many more electrical machines were developed to aid communication. In the 1880s the telephone was invented, and its use quickly spread across the world. By the early 20th century, radio waves (pp. 40-41) were being used to communicate over large distances. Since the 1930s, radio communication has become part of everyday life, and satellites have made worldwide communication faster and easier.

Insulated handle is pressed to send messages

When contact is made, the instrument is ready to receive

Wire connects from here to electromagnet to receive incoming messages

Wire connects from here to receiving station

Wire connects from here to a battery

Morse Key No. 1

MORSE AND HIS CODE

Samuel Morse (1791-1872) was an American artist and scientist who made important contributions to communications. In 1838, he put the Morse code into operation to send messages over long distances via the telegraph. The Morse code is still used today. The letters of the alphabet are each represented by a combination of short and long electrical pulses, called "dots" and "dashes," which are produced on transmitting machines. These pulses can be received in a number of ways. One of the most common is that they activate a sounder, a machine that converts the electrical pulse into long or short beeps. This is Morse Key No. 1, which is simply a switch that sends a dot or a dash when the handle is pressed. This one was used by the Post Office Telegraph service in the UK.

Samuel Morse

Each key represents a letter and another symbol

Space key

TAPPING OUT A MESSAGE

In the 1850s, the Hughes Telegraph was used a great deal, mainly in France. It was invented by David Hughes of Kentucky. The printing wheel, which has the letters of the alphabet, prints a letter on to the printing paper when one of the 28 keys is pressed. In the same motion, electrical contact is made, and a pulse of electrical energy is sent down the telegraph line to an identical machine, which prints the same message.

LINKING PEOPLE
By 1887 over 250,000 homes
and businesses in Europe
and North America were
connected by telephone.

*Pulley wheel
supplies the
energy for the
printing wheel*

*Spring governor
controls the speed
of the printing
wheel*

COMMUNICATION BY TELEPHONE
During the early 1870s, Alexander Graham Bell (1847-1922) worked to develop
an instrument that would convert the vibrations of the human voice into
electrical signals that could be sent over long distances. In February 1876,
he registered his invention, the telephone, with the US Patent Office just a
few hours before another experimenter, Elisha Gray (1835-1901), who had
separately invented a similar machine. This
box telephone is one of Bell's early designs.

*Permanent magnet
is used together
with electromagnet*

*Electromagnet coils produce
magnetism when electricity
flows around them*

*Speaking
and
listening
cone*

*Wires are attached here to
take signals to and from
the telephone*

*Inking wheel
spreads ink on
printing wheel*

*Printing
wheel prints
message on
paper*

*Wheel moves paper
one space after each
letter is printed*

COMMUNICATION BY SATELLITE
The first signal using electromagnetic waves was
sent in the 1890s (pp. 40-41). Developments
since then have been rapid. Words and
pictures can be communicated around the
world by sending energy, in the form of
radio waves, to satellites like this NASA
one in orbit around the Earth. The
satellites then send the energy back
down to Earth, to be received
wherever it is needed. All this can
take place in seconds, and many
messages can be sent through
one satellite at the same time.

*Spool holds
printing paper*

*Highly skilled
workers operated
the telegraph*

Hughes
Telegraph,
c. 1850

Energy in waves

WHEN A PENDULUM SWINGS back and forth, or oscillates, it has a fixed amount of energy, which changes between potential energy at each end of its swing and kinetic energy at the center. The rate of oscillation is the frequency. An oscillating object can pass some or all of its energy onto other objects by a wave motion. For example, when water is forced to oscillate, the energy of the oscillation is spread out to the surrounding water by a wave as each water molecule affects its nearest neighbors. Sound travels in a similar way. In the 1860s, James Clerk Maxwell (1831-1879) found that light waves are traveling oscillations of electromagnetic energy. He also predicted the existence of other electromagnetic waves, which were later demonstrated by Heinrich Hertz (1857-1894).

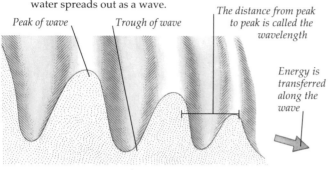

WATER RIPPLES
The energy of a falling drop of water spreads out as a wave.

Peak of wave

Trough of wave

The distance from peak to peak is called the wavelength

Energy is transferred along the wave

THE ANATOMY OF A WAVE
A cross section of a water wave shows its structure. The peaks and troughs occur where water is displaced above or below the normal water level. The height of a peak is called the amplitude of the wave. Amplitude is reduced as the wave travels outward and the energy is spread over larger and larger circles. The water moves up and down, but not along with the wave – only the energy moves outward.

ELECTROMAGNETIC RADIATION
James Clerk Maxwell was a brilliant mathematician and physicist whose work on electromagnetism followed that of Michael Faraday (pp. 22-23). He put Faraday's discoveries into mathematical form, and his calculations suggested that light is an oscillation of energy between electricity and magnetism. His calculations also suggested that other types of electromagnetic waves exist with frequencies higher and lower than that of light. In 1888, the German physicist Heinrich Hertz (pp. 42-43) produced and detected lower-frequency electromagnetic waves in his laboratory, confirming Maxwell's ideas. These are now known as radio waves and are just part of the electromagnetic spectrum (pp. 42-43) that Maxwell had predicted.

Bright and dark patterns caused by interference

LIGHT WAVE EXPERIMENT
This colorful demonstration, known as Newton's rings, suggests that light is a wave motion. This is because the colors are produced by "interference," an effect common to all waves. Two layers of glass are held together with screws, and both pieces reflect light from their surfaces. When two light waves combine, their peaks and troughs reinforce each other in some places and cancel each other out in others. When water waves interfere, the water can become choppy. In the same way, light interference causes bright and dark areas in this experiment.

Screws adjust distance between two layers of glass

Prongs vibrate 440 times each second

Invisible sound wave has a frequency of 440 hertz

Tuning fork produces sound waves as it oscillates

Microphone detects sound waves and converts them into electrical energy

Wires carry electricity to oscilloscope

RADIO WAVES FOR COMMUNICATION

Italian scientist Guglielmo Marconi (1874-1937) was the pioneer of radio communication. He realized that the electromagnetic waves Hertz had discovered could be used to transmit information. On December 11, 1901, Marconi transmitted a signal from Cornwall, UK, to Newfoundland, a distance of about 2,000 miles (3,300 km). Radio soon proved to be a very effective method of communication. Since then, the energy of electromagnetic radiation has been used to carry huge amounts of information, including television pictures.

ENERGY THROUGH THE AIRWAVES

The logo of the RKO broadcasting company shows a radio transmitter sending out its radio waves in every direction.

TRACING THE ENERGY OF SOUND WAVES

When a tuning fork is struck, it oscillates at a definite frequency and disturbs the air at the same frequency. The energy of the disturbance spreads through the air as a sound wave, part of which meets the microphone. In the microphone, the energy of the sound makes a coil of wire oscillate, again at the same frequency. A magnet sits in the middle of the coil of wire, and a small electric current is generated in the coil. Because the coil is moved back and forth, the current changes direction with the same frequency, passing as a wave down the wires to the oscilloscope. The oscilloscope, an instrument commonly used for testing electric circuits, displays the oscillating current on its screen.

Screen is coated with phosphorus, which glows when hit by electrons

Shape of sound wave is traced by an oscillating beam of electrons in the oscilloscope

PULSE DURATION

SWEEP SPEED

PULSE AMPLITUDE

ASTIGMATISM

TIME

FOCUS

BRIGHTNESS

X SHIFT

Y SHIFT

OFF

H.T.

ON

4 K.V.

E.H.T.

8 K.V.

Energy in packets

MANY EXPERIMENTS WITH LIGHT and other forms of electromagnetic radiation (pp. 40-41) suggest that its energy is carried by waves. Electromagnetic waves were discovered mathematically by James Clerk Maxwell, and in the 1880s the experiments of Heinrich Hertz (1857-1894) seemed to prove Maxwell's ideas correct. However, one of Hertz's experiments led him to discover a curious phenomenon now known as the photoelectric effect. It could not be explained by Maxwell's ideas. As well as behaving as a wave, like ripples on a lake, light is made up of particles called photons. Each photon is a packet of energy. This was explained in 1905 by Albert Einstein (pp. 44-45). Other forms of energy come in definite amounts in a similar way, and energy is said to be "quantized." The discovery that energy is quantized dramatically changed our understanding of the Universe.

HERTZ AND HIS EXPERIMENTS

Between 1885 and 1889, the German physicist Heinrich Hertz carried out a series of experiments that confirmed the existence of Maxwell's electromagnetic radiation. During these famous experiments, Hertz noticed that the radiation he had made affected the electrodes in his apparatus in a surprising way (see below). On investigation, this effect could be explained fully only by the fact that the radiation occurs in definite packets.

Air is pumped from sealed glass container

Electromagnetic radiation of known frequencies is allowed into the apparatus through this hole

Electricity is connected to this terminal

Electrodes

DISLODGING ELECTRICITY

Hertz used this equipment to investigate the photoelectric effect. Electricity jumped across the gap at the center. When the gap was enlarged, the electricity stopped, but when electromagnetic radiation fell on the electrodes, the electricity once again jumped the gap. The radiation had dislodged some of the electricity. If the radiation was a continuous wave, all of its frequencies would have this effect, if they were intense enough. But the effect occurred only for radiation above a particular value. This is because the energy comes in packets, each with a definite energy, depending on the frequency of the radiation.

Electricity needs more energy to jump the gap

Electrons are thrown out from atoms in the electrode by the extra energy

Ultraviolet light

Meter measures whether any electricity has jumped

Battery

SHEDDING LIGHT ON THE EXPERIMENT

During the experiment, electricity, with potential energy, is produced by a battery. When the gap is too large, the potential energy is not enough for the electricity to jump the gap. But when ultraviolet light falls on the negative electrode, the electricity is given extra energy. The energy comes in separate bundles called quanta. A quantum of electromagnetic radiation, such as ultraviolet light, is called a photon.

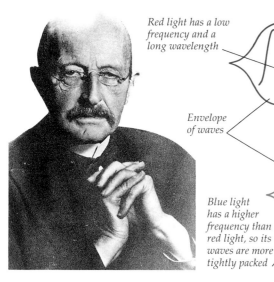

A PHOTON OF RED LIGHT
A photon does not really look like anything, but many people find it useful to think of it as a packet of waves because electromagnetic radiation behaves as waves and particles. The energy of a photon depends only on its frequency.

Red light has a low frequency and a long wavelength

Envelope of waves

Blue light has a higher frequency than red light, so its waves are more tightly packed

A PHOTON OF BLUE LIGHT
The frequency of blue light is higher than that of red light, so a blue wave packet would contain more tightly packed waves. The energy of a photon of blue light is about 0.0000000000000000005 joules; about twice as much as a photon of red light.

LIGHT SPECTRUM
Visible light is just a small portion of the complete spectrum of electromagnetic radiation. All such radiation is identical, except that the photons differ in the energy they carry. Photons of X-rays carry much more energy than those of visible light, and photons of radio waves have much less energy than those of visible light. Prisms separate electromagnetic radiation according to the amount of energy and can be used to analyze the radiation from a hot object.

Visible light is made of a spectrum of colors

PLANCK AND ENERGY LEVELS
In the 1890s, Max Planck was studying the problem of radiation given off by hot objects. This had been a problem for some time because Maxwell's theory of electromagnetic waves could not explain the radiation from hot objects. In 1900, Planck made a bold suggestion. Instead of being allowed any amount of energy as they vibrated, the atoms of matter could have only particular values of energy. So, instead of losing energy continuously as they cool, atoms jump from one energy of vibration down to the next, giving out a definite amount of energy each time. This energy must come in separate packets, or photons. In 1905, Einstein developed this idea to explain the photoelectric effect.

LIGHT FROM SHOOTING STARS
Although they look white, these very hot shooting stars are actually giving off the whole spectrum of visible light, and more. The amount of each frequency present depends on the temperature of the shooting star. This can be explained only by the fact that the radiation comes in packets. The energy of each packet depends on its frequency.

Light-sensitive metal, such as selenium, is exposed to light

Photographer calculates exposure times from the meter reading

Ammeter built into light meter registers electric current

Scheelite in natural light

SHINING ROCKS
Many substances, such as this scheelite, fluoresce under ultraviolet light. This happens when photons of radiation with higher frequency (so higher energy) than visible light fall on them. This gives their atoms more energy. The atoms release this energy again, often in the form of lower-energy photons. These lower-energy photons are often those of visible light. This is one way substances can be made to glow in the dark.

A HELP TO PHOTOGRAPHERS
Light meters, such as this early model, became available in the 1930s. They use the photoelectric effect to measure the intensity of light. The metals in the meter are specially chosen because they are light sensitive, or affected by visible light. Photons of light hit the metal atoms and give up all their energy to electrons, dislodging them from the metal atoms. The electrons can then be measured by a meter that detects current. The brighter the light, the more electrons dislodged, and the greater the current.

Scheelite in ultraviolet light

Mass energy

By the end of the 19th century, scientists thought that energy was well understood. In 1905, Albert Einstein (1879-1955) challenged the accepted view of the world. During that year he wrote three very important articles. One of these explained the photoelectric effect (pp. 42-43), and one involved heat energy (pp. 20-21). The most famous article discussed his Special Theory of Relativity, in which he concentrated on the fact that the speed of light is fixed. He came up with some startling conclusions. One of these is that energy has mass and that mass is therefore a form of energy. Einstein's celebrated equation, $E=mc^2$, describes this mass-energy idea mathematically. The E stands for a change in energy, c is the speed of light, and m is the corresponding mass. According to this idea, when 1 ton is lifted through 3.2 ft (1 m), it gains 0.000000000004 oz (0.0000000001 g). This change in mass is so small that it becomes measurable only when huge amounts of energy are involved, such as in nuclear reactions (pp. 46-47).

Water presses on vanes as it hits them

Some of the water's kinetic energy is given to the vanes

Water pressure

Pressure is caused by photons hitting vanes

Light pressure

Some of the light's energy is given to the vanes

LIGHT WEIGHT
Even before Einstein's idea of mass-energy, it was realized that light falling on an object exerts a pressure on the object, just as water from a hosepipe exerts pressure on the vanes of a water wheel. The first person to realize this was a Russian physicist, Pëtr Lebedev (1866-1912). He calculated the amount of pressure that light exerted and found that it depended on the speed of light and the amount of energy the light carried. This fits in with Einstein's equation $E=mc^2$. Because light has mass, it must be affected by gravity. Of course, light exerts so little pressure that its effect would not be noticed in day-to-day life.

Pëtr Lebedev

HEAT HAS MASS
During the 18th century, when natural forces such as heat were thought to be carried by fluids (pp. 18-19), many experiments were carried out to discover whether heat has mass. Scientists of that time found that heat has no mass. They were wrong, but it is not surprising that they came to this conclusion. The amount of mass gained by an object as it gains heat energy is tiny – far too small to be measured even by the most accurate scales. The demonstration shown here is exaggerated to help explain that energy has mass.

Weights are at the same temperature

Masses of the weights are equal, so they balance

1 BALANCED MASSES
These scales are balanced, showing that the masses of the two metal weights are equal. The weights are at the same temperature, so they have the same amount of heat energy, and their atoms and molecules have the same average speed.

EINSTEIN AND RELATIVITY

German physicist Albert Einstein was born the year that James Clerk Maxwell (pp. 40-41) died. Although he did not do well in school, Einstein was a genius who was to change the face of science. Before Einstein, energy was energy and mass was mass. But Einstein's Special Theory of Relativity, first published in his article "On the Electrodynamics of Moving Bodies," suggested that energy and mass are directly linked. The truth of Einstein's insight has since been proved many times. He won a Nobel Prize in 1921 for his services to physics.

Metal weight gains heat energy from the flame

Tarnishing is caused by oxygen combining with the metal

Bunsen burner provides heat energy

MAKING MATTER

This colorful picture shows the trails left by tiny particles in the reaction chamber of a large particle accelerator, a machine used to produce nuclear reactions. Energy, in the form of two photons of electromagnetic radiation, enters at the right-hand side. Each one suddenly becomes matter in the form of an electron (green) and a positron (red). The electrons and positrons are electrically charged and spiral in the chamber's strong magnetic field. The long green line is another electron that has been knocked off an atom.

2 ADDING ENERGY, ADDING MASS

One of the metal weights from the scales is taken away and heated by a Bunsen burner. As the metal weight heats up, it gains heat energy. This increases the average speed of its atoms and molecules. It also increases the metal weight's mass, because energy has mass.

FASTER THAN THE SPEED OF LIGHT

Ever since the discovery that light travels at 186,000 miles/sec (300,000 km/sec), people have dreamed of traveling at the same speed or faster. In the television series, "Star Trek," the *Starship Enterprise* frequently travels faster than the speed of light. This is not really possible, because the speed of light is the speed limit in the Universe. The faster an object travels, the more kinetic energy, and mass, it gains. At light speed, an object would become so heavy that an infinite amount of energy would be needed to move it.

Cool weight is unchanged

3 ENERGY IMBALANCE

When the metal weight is placed back on to the scale, it no longer balances with the other weight. This is because it contains extra energy in the form of heat. In this demonstration the scales have been tipped to suggest an increase in mass, although in reality the increase is so small it could not be detected in this way.

Metal weight that was heated has gained heat energy, so it has also gained mass

Scales no longer balance

Energy from the nucleus

FROM THE EARLY 1900s ON, scientists knew that the atoms that make up matter consist of tiny nuclei surrounded by electrons. The nucleus was found to be made up of tightly packed particles, which were named protons and neutrons. Electrons are held in the atom by electromagnetism (pp. 22-23), but the forces that hold the nucleus together are far greater. Those forces are the key to nuclear power. There are two main ways by which this energy can be released: fission and fusion. In each case, a reaction occurs in the nuclei of atoms, and the matter left after the reaction has a little less mass than before. The "lost" mass is changed into energy (pp. 44-45), some of which is released as high-energy electromagnetic radiation (pp. 40-41). The rest becomes heat (pp. 20-21), which can be used to destroy things, in nuclear weapons, or to generate electricity, in nuclear reactors.

FERMI'S REACTION
On December 2, 1942 the first artificial nuclear chain reaction was produced by a team of scientists led by the brilliant Italian physicist Enrico Fermi (1901-1954). The successful experiment took place in a squash court at the University of Chicago. A chain reaction works a bit like lighting a match. The heat from the friction of striking the match allows some of the atoms to burn, releasing more heat, which keeps the reaction going.

BALANCING THE REACTIONS
It is possible to measure the masses of the particles involved in a nuclear reaction. One common fission reaction involves a nucleus of uranium splitting into nuclei of barium and krypton. The reaction begins when one neutron bombards the uranium. During the reaction three neutrons are released. When the mass of the uranium nucleus before the reaction is compared to the mass of the barium and krypton afterward, it is found that some mass has disappeared. The missing mass has been converted into energy. In this example the mass lost is less than one thousandth of the mass present at the beginning of the reaction, and it is converted into just $\frac{1}{30,000,000,000,000}$ joule (J) for each atom of uranium. However, atoms are so small that if 2.2 lbs (1 kg) of uranium was completely "fissioned" in this way, more than 10 million million J of energy would be released.

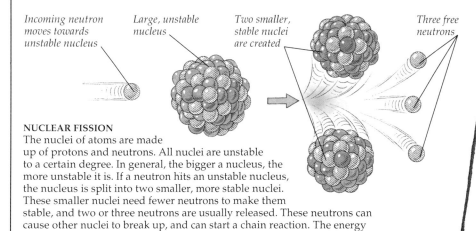

Incoming neutron moves towards unstable nucleus

Large, unstable nucleus

Two smaller, stable nuclei are created

Three free neutrons

NUCLEAR FISSION
The nuclei of atoms are made up of protons and neutrons. All nuclei are unstable to a certain degree. In general, the bigger a nucleus, the more unstable it is. If a neutron hits an unstable nucleus, the nucleus is split into two smaller, more stable nuclei. These smaller nuclei need fewer neutrons to make them stable, and two or three neutrons are usually released. These neutrons can cause other nuclei to break up, and can start a chain reaction. The energy needed to hold all of the particles together in the new nuclei is less than that required in the original nucleus, and the "spare" energy is released, mostly as heat.

Two different versions, or "isotopes," of hydrogen nucleus

Nucleus of helium has two protons

Free neutron

NUCLEAR FUSION
At very high temperatures, small nuclei can be fused together to make larger ones. This is what happens at the heart of stars such as the Sun (pp. 48-49). If the new nucleus needs less energy to hold it together than the old ones, energy will be released and mass will be "lost." The most common fusion reaction is the one that builds a nucleus of helium from nuclei of hydrogen. This reaction has been carried out in special fusion reactors, and many people hope that it will be the energy source of the future. It would be clean, safe, and there would be no radioactive waste.

Free neutron to bombard uranium nucleus

Uranium nucleus

HOW BIG IS A NUCLEUS?
There are a staggering 10,000 million million million molecules of sugar in this cube. Each molecule consists of 24 atoms. But most of an atom, and of the sugar cube, is empty space. This is because the nucleus of an atom takes up only one 1,000-million-millionth of the space of the atom. If a nucleus were the size of a sugar cube, an atom would be about 0.6 miles (1 km) across.

TESTING THE HYDROGEN BOMB AT BIKINI

In 1939 the great physicist Albert Einstein sent a letter to President Franklin D. Roosevelt. Einstein suggested that a nuclear chain reaction could be used to generate electricity, or to make a bomb. Einstein thought that a bomb would never actually be used, but instead would act as a "deterrent" in World War II. However, Einstein's suggestions were investigated, and since then many countries have acquired nuclear weapons. This explosion of a hydrogen bomb was a test carried out on the Bikini atoll in the Pacific Ocean in 1956. Hydrogen bombs use uncontrolled nuclear fusion to release huge amounts of energy. Atom bombs use nuclear fission.

THE EFFECTS OF A NUCLEAR WEAPON

The first atomic bomb explosion was over Hiroshima, Japan, during World War II. It killed 80,000 people immediately, and another 60,000 died within a year from radiation sickness, which results from changes in living cells due to radiation from nuclear explosions. Atomic bombs release intense heat, great enough to fuse soil to the side of this rice bowl.

Soil fused to the side of the bowl

Different parts of the soil took different forms

Rice bowl from Hiroshima

Heat exchanger

Reactor core

Moderator

Gas or liquid coolant takes heat away from core

Turbine generator

Condenser turns steam back into water

Steam is released from the cooling tower

Electricity travels down wires to be distributed

Three "spare" neutrons

Barium nucleus

Krypton nucleus

Mass has been lost in the reaction, so the right-hand pan weighs less than the left-hand pan

GENERATING ELECTRICITY WITH NUCLEAR ENERGY

Using fission, energy from the nucleus can be used to generate electricity. All nuclear power stations have a reactor core, a heat exchanger, and turbines. The core is where the nuclear reactions take place. In a reactor core, nuclear reactions are carefully controlled by the insertion of materials called "moderators," which absorb free neutrons that would otherwise increase the rate of the chain reaction. The heat exchanger takes heat from the core to a supply of water. The water is turned into high-pressure steam, and the steam drives the turbine generator to produce electricity.

THE IDEAL ENERGY SOURCE?

Nuclear power stations release no dangerous fumes during normal operation. However, after fission occurs, the "spent" fuel stays dangerously radioactive for thousands of years and must be buried deep underground or at sea. At this nuclear waste dump in Washington State, a Geiger counter is being used to monitor the radiation being released. Another problem with nuclear power is the danger of accidents. These can have devastating effects, like the disasters at Chernobyl, in the Ukraine (p. 57), Three Mile Island, Pennsylvania, and Windscale, UK.

Energy from the Sun

THE SUN HAS ALWAYS been of great importance to people by providing heat and light. But early people could not have known the importance of the Sun as the provider of practically all the energy the Earth receives. Without the energy that reaches the Earth through space, there would be no plant or animal life on the planet. The energy of most alternative energy sources (pp. 58-59), such as wind energy, originally comes from the Sun. It is also the Sun's energy, stored in plants millions of years ago, that is released when fossil fuels (pp. 54-55) are burned. The Earth receives only a tiny fraction of the huge amount of energy released by the Sun. This energy comes from fusion reactions (pp. 46-47) deep at its center. The Sun emits such vast amounts of energy, which has mass (pp. 46-47), that it is getting lighter by millions of tons every second.

BASKING IN THE SUN
Reptiles like this sand lizard are coldblooded. This means they cannot regulate their body temperature. Many coldblooded creatures react to changes in temperature by becoming more or less active. This shows how important the Sun's heating effect is to such animals. The sand lizard relies on the energy it gets directly from the Sun, to warm its body.

Lens focuses the sunlight

Lens faces the Sun

Metal stand for lens

FREE ELECTRICITY FROM THE SUN
When light hits the special chemicals in a solar cell, electrical potential energy, or voltage, is produced. A cell like this one from the communications satellite *Telstar* will produce only a small voltage, but a large number of cells wired together provides all the energy needed to receive and transmit signals from and to the Earth. It is possible to use solar cells on Earth as an alternative source of energy (pp. 58-59), but they are better suited to provide the smaller amounts of energy needed by small spacecraft.

Cells contain crystals of silicon, which convert solar energy into electricity

SUNLIGHT AND SUN HEAT
A convex lens, such as this burning lens, can focus sunlight to a point, causing paper to burn. The Sun radiates a range of frequencies in addition to visible light. Infrared is electromagnetic radiation (pp. 40-41) just outside the visible range. Although it cannot be seen by human eyes, its effects can often be felt as heat. The frequencies of infrared radiation match those that start atoms and molecules vibrating. This means they heat up, and their heat can be enough to start a reaction. Burning lenses were often used by chemists to help reactions to occur.

Paper is scorched where sunlight shines

A FUSION OF IDEAS
In 1938, the German physicist Hans Bethe (b. 1906) first suggested that nuclear fusion (pp. 46-47) might be what provides the energy of stars such as the Sun. He was correct, but a better understanding of the processes involved has been the result of work by many great scientists. Bethe was rewarded for his discoveries in 1967 with the Nobel Prize for Physics.

LOOKING INSIDE THE SUN

The Sun is made up of a number of layers. The conditions in each layer are very different. At the very center is the intensely hot core, where most of the energy of the Sun is produced. The energy is released by fusion (pp. 46-47). For fusion to take place, a very high temperature is required. The temperature in the core of the Sun is known to be about 27,000,000°F (15,000,000°C). The diameter of the Sun is about 3 billion times the width of this book, and its own gravity crams everything together at its center, causing huge pressures that result in heat being generated. Once started, the fusion reactions themselves release heat, which helps them to keep going. The energy released at the core travels outward from atom to atom, first by radiation and then by convection (pp. 26-27), until it reaches the part of the Sun that is visible, the photosphere. Outside the photosphere is the chromosphere, which is something like an atmosphere. It takes thousands of years for energy to travel from the core to the photosphere.

Sunspots move around the photosphere and seem to come and go in a cycle of about 11 years

A PROMINENT FEATURE

Often about one-third of the diameter of the Sun, huge eruptions of hot gases like this are called solar prominences. They seem to be linked with sunspots and the Sun's magnetic energy. Sunspots are slightly cooler areas on the surface of the Sun and are seen as darker patches. Prominences often arc between two sunspots. During a solar eclipse, as the Moon passes between the Sun and the Earth, large prominences become visible to the eye.

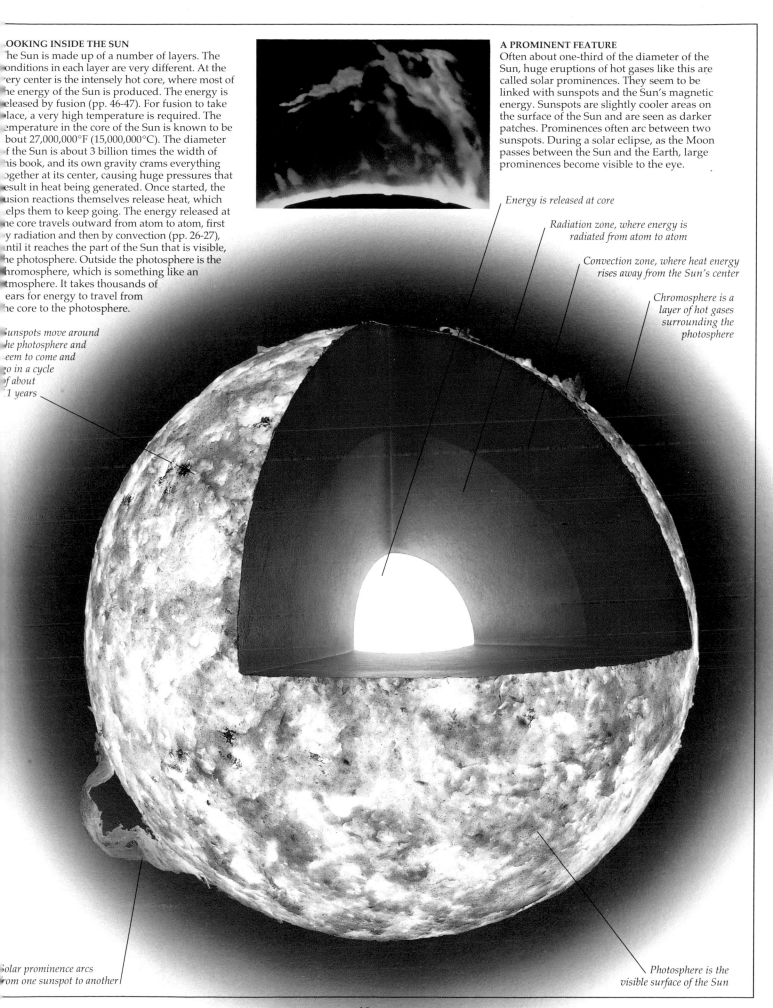

Energy is released at core

Radiation zone, where energy is radiated from atom to atom

Convection zone, where heat energy rises away from the Sun's center

Chromosphere is a layer of hot gases surrounding the photosphere

Solar prominence arcs from one sunspot to another

Photosphere is the visible surface of the Sun

Photosynthesis

WHEN ENERGY from the Sun (pp. 48-49) falls on plant leaves, it can be stored as chemical potential energy (pp. 14-15) in plants. This is photosynthesis – the process by which light energy is taken into plant cells and stored as it separates oxygen from water. The discovery of photosynthesis was gradual. Toward the end of the 18th century, Joseph Priestley (1733-1804), an English chemist, studied the gases involved in burning. He discovered that plants change the quality of the air around them. They do this by taking in what is now known as carbon dioxide and giving out what is now known as oxygen. In 1779 the Dutch scientist Jan Ingenhousz (1730-1799) discovered that this happens only when a plant is exposed to light. By the end of the 19th century, photosynthesis was understood in terms of energy. It is a process vitally important to life on Earth. Without photosynthesis, there would be no food (pp. 52-53) for animals or humans. Photosynthesis in plants living millions of years ago converted solar energy into the chemical energy available when fossil fuels (pp. 54-55) are burned.

MAKING SUGAR

In 1864, a German chemist called Julius Sachs (1832-1897) discovered which chemicals are involved in photosynthesis. He found that carbon dioxide taken in by plants is combined with hydrogen from water, which is made of oxygen and hydrogen. The energy for this reaction comes from light falling on the plant. The hydrogen and carbon dioxide join to form glucose, a type of sugar that is the food for the plant. Some of the glucose is made into starch, which is a good energy store. The oxygen that is separated from the water is released by the plant.

The carbon dioxide in the jar is gradually replaced by oxygen

Plant cells in the leaves take in carbon dioxide and give out oxygen

Water stops the gases from escaping

Gas jar filled with carbon dioxide

Candle will not burn in the carbon dioxide

PRIESTLEY'S EXPERIMENT

In the 1770s, Joseph Priestley was investigating gases. At that time, it was believed that burning involved the release of a substance named "phlogiston." When a candle burned, for example, it was thought to be releasing "phlogisticated air." This was a gas that did not allow anything to burn in it and was poisonous to animals. Priestley was surprised to discover that if a plant was placed in the gas, it could "de-phlogisticate" the air, making it breathable again. Priestley discovered the two gases that are now known as carbon dioxide and oxygen.

1 PHLOGISTICATED AIR
Burning will not occur in carbon dioxide gas, and the gas can be deadly if breathed. Priestley obtained samples of the gas (he called it "phlogisticated" air) by burning a small candle in a jar and by collecting the gas as a by-product from the brewery next door to his home. It is now known that carbon dioxide is also released as a result of respiration (pp. 52-53), the reverse of photosynthesis.

Water trough

2 PHOTOSYNTHESIS IN ACTION
Priestley left plants in jars full of carbon dioxide. Although he did not know it, the plants were photosynthesizing and taking in the carbon dioxide they needed to make the chemicals necessary to survive and grow. During photosynthesis the plants gave out oxygen gas, which then filled the jars. Priestley experimented with the gas and realized that it had very different properties from the carbon dioxide gas.

Small candle used to fill a jar with carbon dioxide, and to test the gas in a jar

WHAT HAPPENS INSIDE A PLANT CELL

All the complex chemical reactions involved in photosynthesis take place inside the cells of plants in parts called chloroplasts. Chloroplasts contain special chemicals, such as chlorophyll, that absorb energy from light. In a split second the energy passes quickly through the chloroplast as tiny currents of electricity, separating atoms of oxygen from water molecules and joining together the hydrogen and the carbon dioxide to form glucose. The glucose is then transported around the plant to wherever it is needed, by a network of tubes called the phloem.

Ivy leaves

Green leaves contain a large proportion of chlorophyll

Pink leaves contain a mixture of pigments, including xanthophyll and Beta-carotene

Chloroplasts in green plants contain chlorophyll

Nucleus controls the activities of the cell

Endoplasmic reticulum transports nutrients within the cell

Green plant leaf

Vacuole stores sap

Cell wall

Coleus leaves

GREEN LEAVES AND PINK LEAVES

Inside the chloroplasts in plant cells, there are special chemicals that absorb the light falling on the plant. These chemicals absorb only particular colors of light, reflecting all other colors. The most common of these chemicals is chlorophyll, which reflects green light, giving most plants a green color. However, the mixture of chemicals inside chloroplasts can vary, and some plants have differently colored leaves as a result. These other chemicals work in the same way as chlorophyll. During autumn, the chlorophyll in the leaves of green leafy trees is broken down, revealing the colors of the other chemicals present in the leaves.

3 BURNING PLANT GAS (below)
Priestley found that candles burn very well in the gas produced by the plants. Of course, oxygen is used up in burning, so the candles eventually would be extinguished once again. However, if a plant was placed in the jar once this had happened, it would replace the carbon dioxide with oxygen. In photosynthesis, energy is taken in by the plant and oxygen is released. In burning, oxygen is used up and energy is released.

Oxygen is combined with carbon, present in the wax, to produce carbon dioxide

The candle burns well in the oxygen, releasing energy as heat and light

The mouse breathes in the oxygen that was produced by the green plant

REACHING FOR THE LIGHT

Light is vital to all plants, so plants need to be exposed to as much of it as possible. This is why plants bend towards light. There is a huge variety of plants which photosynthesize. Each has developed its own way of guaranteeing a share of the incoming sunlight. For example, the giant redwood trees of North America can grow to a height of more than 350 feet (100 m). Other plants have evolved to grow in desert or tundra conditions, using the light energy available in places where most other plants would not survive.

4 BREATHING PLANT GAS
Priestley also found that the gas produced by the plants was breathable. When he placed an animal, such as a mouse, in a bell jar that contained oxygen, it was able to breathe normally. Like humans, animals need to breathe oxygen in order to burn food within the body to obtain energy.

Energy from food

ALL LIVING THINGS need energy for a variety of activities, such as growing, moving, and keeping warm. Some, such as plants, capture energy – usually from sunlight – and store it as chemical potential energy (pp. 14-15). Other living things that cannot capture energy in this way have to make use of the energy stored elsewhere. They get this energy by feeding on other animals or plants. Humans eat plants and animals to obtain the energy they need. The food that humans eat is burned, or oxidized, inside the body during digestion. In a similar way, fossil fuels, such as coal and oil, are oxidized when they are ignited. Oxygen from the air combines with a substance that is burned. When fossil fuels burn, they release heat and light in flames. When food is burned in the body, chemical energy is released. Different types of food store and release different amounts of energy. Fat, for example, is a more concentrated energy store than sugar.

SPINACH FOR ENERGY
Popeye, a cartoon character created in the 1930s, becomes incredibly strong when he eats spinach. He was originally intended to promote healthy eating for children. Spinach contains not only energy but also vitamins and minerals, which are other essential parts of food.

FEEDING THEMSELVES
All organisms that make their own food – like these phytoplankton – are called autotrophic, meaning self-feeding. Most autotrophic organisms are plants, which take energy from sunlight by photosynthesis (pp. 50-51).

Food energy values

When food is burned in an animal's body, the chemical potential energy stored within it is released. Different foods release different amounts of energy. The amount of energy released by foods is usually measured in kilocalories (kcal) or joules (J, pp. 36-37) – 1 kcal is equal to about 4,200 J, and is also called a Calorie. There are three groups of energy, giving chemicals in food. They are carbohydrates, fats, and proteins.

ENERGY FROM FRUIT
Fruit such as these grapes contains natural sugars that provide energy. Each grape provides about 1 kcal. If more sugar is eaten than the body needs, the sugar is converted into fat, a good store of food energy, so that it can be used another time.

ENERGY FROM SUGAR
In the middle of the 19th century, French physiologist Claude Bernard discovered how large carbohydrate molecules are converted to smaller molecules of glucose in the liver. Food containing carbohydrates must first be broken down into glucose, a type of sugar, before its energy can be obtained. The glucose is carried from the liver around the bloodstream and combined with oxygen, releasing energy in a process called "aerobic respiration." In this process, glucose and oxygen become water and carbon dioxide. This is the reverse of photosynthesis (pp. 50-51), in which glucose is made from water and carbon dioxide, and energy is taken in by a plant.

Potatoes contain about 90 Calories per 3 1/2 oz (100 g)

ENERGY FROM POTATOES
This potato contains a lot of starch, which stores the energy that a new plant needs to begin growing. Starch molecules must be broken down in the body into simple sugar molecules before their energy can be released.

Grapes contain 60 Calories per 3 1/2 oz (100 g)

Grain contains about 300 Calories per 3 1/2 oz (100 g)

ENERGY FROM SEEDS
Seeds, such as these sunflower seeds, contain most of their energy in fats. Many seeds can be eaten whole, and many types are also crushed to release fats in the form of oils, which can be used in cooking.

Sunflower seeds contain about 330 Calories per 3 1/2 oz (100 g)

ENERGY FROM MEAT
Meat is a good source of energy, and much of its energy is stored in fat. But meat is not a very efficient energy source. For example, only a small amount of the energy taken in by a living chicken can be obtained by someone who eats it.

Roast chicken contains about 300 Calories per 3 1/2 oz (100 g)

ENERGY FROM GRAIN
Grain is a good source of energy because it is a direct store of the energy of photosynthesis. This type of wheat is grown to be fed to animals, such as cattle. Other types are often ground into flour for human consumption in products such as bread.

The Sun

Some of the Sun's energy is captured by autotrophic organisms

Energy in living things eventually becomes heat, which goes into the atmosphere

Decomposers use the energy stored in dead organisms

Some animals feed on the autotrophic organisms

Some animals feed on other animals

Test tube holds water

Clamp holds test tube

Thermometer registers the heat energy that the burning peanut has transferred to the water

Water heats as peanut burns

Flame leaves a layer of soot on the test tube

Burning peanut

ENERGY IN A FOOD CHAIN

Because energy cannot be created or destroyed (pp. 24-25), the energy in food is easily traced back to its source, the Sun (pp. 48-49). When the Sun's energy falls on autotrophic organisms, some of it is stored in fats, proteins, and carbohydrates in their bodies. When these organisms are eaten, some of the energy they contain is passed on to the animals that eat them. Some of this energy, in turn, is passed on to meat-eating animals when they eat the animals from the previous stage. At each stage of the food chain, some energy escapes as the heat produced by living things.

ENERGY FOR LIFE

All of the energy needed to move this athlete is provided by the food he has eaten. Once food has been processed in the stomach and intestines, it is transported around the body in the blood, to carry out the processes of life. Energy is used in many ways in the body, for instance, to send messages through nerves to the muscles to make the muscles work and to keep warm.

TOO MUCH ENERGY

The amount of energy a person needs each day depends on how active they are. If a person takes in more fats and carbohydrates than they need, they will be stored in the body so that their energy can be used in the future. Excess carbohydrates are converted to fats in the liver, and they are stored with excess fats beneath the skin.

BURNING A PEANUT

This simple experiment shows the amount of energy available in one peanut. The heat energy released by the burning peanut warms the water in the test tube. If the amount of water is known and the temperature rise is measured using the thermometer, the energy supplied to the water can be calculated. The result of this experiment will not be very accurate because much of the heat escapes to the air, or heats the test tube. A more accurate result can be obtained using an enclosed container, so that no heat is lost to the air. This is what happens in a bomb calorimeter (see right).

Thermocouple inside the bomb measures temperature

Bomb contains water

Red button sends a brief pulse of electricity through the food sample to ignite it in the bomb

Knob allows more oxygen to enter as oxygen is used

Galvanometer displays electric current

Dial shows pressure of oxygen fed into bomb

Ballistic bomb calorimeter

BURNING FOOD IN A BOMB CALORIMETER

Food energy values were first measured using calorimeters (pp. 20-21) like this one. Food is placed in a metal container called the bomb (top left). The food is then ignited by passing electricity through it. As the food burns, it releases energy, and this warms the water passing around it. The rise in temperature can then be measured and converted into kilocalories or joules. Food scientists can also learn how much energy is available from a particular food by measuring how much carbohydrate, protein, and fat the food contains, because the energy values of these food groups are well known.

Fossil fuels

Coal, oil, and natural gas are called fossil fuels. They were formed by the action of bacteria and the pressure of the Earth on the remains of tiny organisms that lived millions of years ago. The energy originally came from the Sun and was stored as chemical potential energy (pp. 14-15) by photosynthesis (pp. 50-51). Coal was the first fossil fuel to be used on a large scale. Raw coal can be burned to provide heat. When coal is heated in a closed vessel without burning, it produces a gas that can be used as fuel. This "coal gas" gave a convenient supply of energy to homes during the 19th century and part of the 20th. "Natural gas" is similar to coal gas. It is often found near oil, which is the fossil fuel that dominates the 20th century. From oil comes gasoline and other fuels, which can be burned to release their fossil energy. Once burned, fossil fuels cannot be used again, and the gases released by burning fossil fuels can pollute the Earth (pp. 56-57). For these reasons, it is important to use fossil fuels efficiently.

COLLECTING OIL
In some places oil seeps from rocks called "oil shale." This type of oil is "crude oil," and it has been collected at its source and used for centuries. The oil was once commonly used for lighting, but it was never ideal because when it burns it becomes smelly and smoky.

Steam condenses on the glass vessel

MAKING COAL GAS
Coal is a mixture of many different substances. When it is heated, it breaks down into those substances. In this glass vessel, coal is being heated and is releasing coal gas. This gas is being burned at the open end of the vessel. Coal gas is made mainly of hydrogen and methane – the other substances that make up coal remain as solids or thick liquids. Both of these gases burn well, combining with oxygen in the air. As they burn, they release energy that originally came from the Sun. The energy is released as heat and light in the flame. This is why coal gas was used mainly for heating and lighting in streets, homes, and factories.

Lumps of coal are heated, but not burned

Filter prevents the flames from coming into contact with the glass vessel

Bunsen burner flame provides heat energy

Clamp holds the glass vessel away from the flame so it does not overheat

ANCIENT FOREST
About 300 million years ago much of the Earth was covered with swamps and forests, full of plants. These plants were a natural store of chemical energy from photosynthesis. When the plants died, some of them were buried. Under the right conditions they slowly turned into coal over millions of years.

HOW OIL AND GAS ARE FORMED

Oil has been used on a large scale only since it was first drilled in Pennsylvania in 1859. Natural gas – made mainly of methane – has replaced coal gas because it is more convenient and the same volume releases more energy. Oil and natural gas are usually found together.

1 SUN AND SEA
Like coal, the story of the formation of oil and gas begins millions of years ago when the Sun's energy was stored in tiny marine organisms, such as algae and plankton. Instead of decaying in the usual way when they died, they were buried in layers of sediment, such as sand and salt.

Sea

Millions of tiny marine organisms

Older layers of sediment

Lower layer of rock

2 BACTERIAL ACTION
Over millions of years the chemicals that made up the organisms were converted into oil and natural gas as bacteria and the pressure of more layers of sediment broke them down. The pressure of the moving rocks of the Earth caused the layers to be "folded" or broken. The oil and natural gas often collected in the resulting shapes.

Marine organisms are buried in layers of sediment

New layers are constantly being formed

Layers of rock and sediment are folded by huge pressures as the Earth shifts

3 RISING ENERGY
Oil and natural gas are less dense than water, so they can rise through "permeable" rocks, which are not solid. They then collect underneath an "impermeable," or solid, layer of rock called a caprock. By studying rock formations, the site of oil and natural gas can be predicted with great accuracy.

Natural gas rig

Oil rig

Natural gas site

Oil site

Both fuels collect under caprock

Gas and oil have seeped up through layers of permeable rock

When the coal gas is lit, a flame is produced

Coal gas travels down the neck of the vessel

THE FIRST COMMERCIAL GAS WORKS
Coal gas was investigated as long ago as the 16th century. People believed that the gas had magical powers, and its potential as a useful fuel was not realized. It was not until the end of the 18th century that people used coal gas for lighting. The Scottish engineer William Murdock (1754-1839) was the first person to use gas lighting on a large scale. He was investigating how to make tar from heated coal, and he used the gas that was produced to light the factory where he worked. Soon, other factories were lit by gas, and it was not long before coal gas became a common form of lighting in cities. The coal was heated in large "retorts" like the one shown here. It was kept in containers with "floating roofs," which rose and fell as the amount of gas in the container changed.

HOW TO FIND THE CALORIFIC VALUE
It is often necessary to find out how much energy is available in fossil fuels. For example, engineers need to know the "energy content" – or calorific value – of a fuel that powers an engine. A calorimeter (pp. 20-21) can be used to discover the calorific value of a given fuel. The gas calorimeter shown here was designed by the British scientist Charles Boys (1855-1944). A steady supply of gas is burned inside, and this heats a steady supply of water. By measuring the temperature rise in the water, the calorific value of the burning gas can be calculated. Thirty-four cubic feet (1 cubic m) of coal gas releases about 19 million joules (pp. 36-37). The same volume of natural gas releases about twice as much energy.

Small microscope allows accurate readings to be taken

Thermometer measures the temperature of water leaving calorimeter

Thermometer measures the temperature of water entering calorimeter

Water flows in through this tap

Water flows out of this tap

Gas enters the apparatus through this tap

Gas is stored here

Gas from retort flows to store in pipe

Simple crane hoists basket in and out

Basket holds coal

Coal is heated in retorts

Heat from fire circulates around the retort

Water acts as a seal to keep the gas in

Gas from retort enters storage through this pipe

Gas is delivered through this pipe

Energy on a global scale

During the 20th century, energy has become much more easily available. Most of the energy comes from the burning of fossil fuels (pp. 54-55). When burned, fossil fuels release substances such as carbon dioxide and smoke into the air. Such substances are not harmful in small amounts, but the demand for energy is so great that millions of tons are released each year. This causes air pollution, which has a worldwide effect. It is not known exactly how much fossil fuel is left for people to use, but it is known that the supply will not last forever. The developed nations of the world use fossil fuels at an incredible rate, mostly for transportation (pp. 30-31) and to generate electricity (pp. 32-33). Nuclear power (pp. 46-47) is being used in increasing amounts to help satisfy the huge demand for energy. The nuclear fuels could last many hundreds of years, even if the demand increases. However, nuclear power creates problems, because nuclear fission leaves radioactive waste. It can also be the cause of harmful accidents.

TERMITES AND METHANE
Many animals, such as termites, make methane gas in their digestive systems. Although termites are small, there are so many of them that the methane they produce affects the quality of the air on a global scale. In a similar way, the use of energy by the human race is causing changes in the air, often by pollution, with gases such as carbon dioxide.

NUCLEAR DISASTER
On April 26, 1986, a nuclear reactor (pp. 46-47) in a power station at Chernobyl, in the Ukraine (bottom right quarter), caught fire. It released huge amounts of radioactivity, which has harmful and long-term effects on all life. This map of the globe shows one way in which the huge demand for energy can have global effects. The pink areas on the map received radioactive contamination as winds carried the effects of the disaster around the globe.

1960 fossil fuel consumption

1,100,000,000 tons used in 1960

41,000,000,000 tons of known reserves

3,000,000,000 tons used in 1990

142,000,000,000 tons of known reserves

1990 fossil fuel consumption

THE RETURN OF MUSCLE POWER
These police officers in Seattle use bicycles rather than cars to get around their beat in the center of the city. Not only does this save energy and decrease pollution, but the officers are also able to get from place to place more quickly than in the cars that clog the city streets. By cycling, walking, and using public transport such as buses, the amount of fuel used for transport can be vastly reduced.

FOSSIL FUELS IN RESERVE
Each year, more oil and natural gas are found and brought up from underground to be burned to release energy. But just how long will the reserves of oil and gas last? In 1960, 40 billion tons of oil and gas were known to exist underground. At the rate they were being used that year across the world, the reserve was estimated to last about 40 years. By 1990, much more oil and gas had been discovered, but the rate at which it was used had also increased. As with the 1960 figures, the 1990 reserve was estimated to last for about 40 years.

The Sun's energy comes to the Earth at a nearly constant rate

The US uses about one-third of the total available energy but has only one-twentieth of the Earth's population

Some Scandinavian countries obtain much of their energy from hydroelectric power

Most of the fossil fuels used by the world's population is obtained from the Middle East

Use more than 200,000,000,000 J per capita each year

Use 50-200,000,000,000 J per capita each year

Use less than 50,000,000,000 J per capita each year

Each person in India uses an average of about 3,000,000,000 J each year

HOW MUCH ENERGY PEOPLE USE

This map shows the differences in energy use between the developed and the less-developed countries of the world. In developed countries, energy is obtained mainly from fossil fuels. In many less-developed countries, people still depend on muscle energy for their needs. Because people in developed countries have more vehicles and electrical appliances, they use more energy than people living in the less-developed countries.

THE LIVING EARTH

In 1979, the British scientist James Lovelock put forward the idea that the Earth and all life on it is one huge living organism. He named the organism Gaia, after the Greek Earth goddess. This picture shows Lovelock with a statue of the goddess Gaia. He suggested that Gaia is responsible for keeping the conditions in the sea and on the land right for Gaia to carry on living. Now that the population of Earth and its energy use have grown so large, humans can affect land, sea, and air in ways that throw Gaia off balance.

The amount of energy in reserve is falling as energy use increases

Humans can control their energy use

INFLOW AND OUTFLOW

Imagine the Earth as a container, into which flows the energy from the Sun (pp. 48-49), and out of which flows the energy used by human beings, which ends up as useless heat energy. When fossil fuels were formed, the container was full. For the past few hundred years, humans have used the energy from fossil fuels at an incredible rate. The tap at the bottom of the container is being opened more and more. One day the store of energy from fossil fuels will run out. Only by closing the tap a little, and by making more use of the Sun's energy flowing in, will the human race avoid a worldwide energy crisis.

Earth's store of energy is mostly fossil fuels

Humans use energy at a rate of about 1,000 million million million J each year

Alternative energy

THE DEMAND FOR ENERGY in the past hundred years has been incredible. There are problems with using fossil fuels on as large a scale as they are used at present (pp. 56-57). These problems can be dealt with in two ways. First, people can make better use of the energy fossil fuels supply (pp. 60-61) by being less wasteful. Second, people can use energy from alternative sources. One alternative to fossil fuels is nuclear energy (pp. 46-47), but this has problems of its own. Solar, hydroelectric, and geothermal energy are all examples of energy sources that are renewable, or that will not run out, unlike fossil fuels.

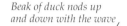

Behind the duck, the water is calm, because the energy of the wave has been absorbed

Beak of duck nods up and down with the wave

SOLAR PRINTING PRESS

There have been many ingenious inventions to provide a supply of energy in case of a shortage of fossil fuels. The French engineer Abel Pifre invented this solar printing press, which he demonstrated in Paris in 1882. Sunlight that shone into its $10\frac{1}{2}$ ft (3.5 m) diameter concave mirror was focused onto a steam boiler to heat the water inside. The steam that was produced then powered an engine that in turn provided the energy for the printing press. On the day of Pifre's demonstration, his press printed more than 2,000 copies of a special publication that he called the *Soleil-Journal*, or *Sun Journal*.

Nozzle through which jet of water flows

Pairs of buckets stop the water, taking most of its kinetic energy

Water-pressure gauge

Cutaway section shows buckets

Flywheel

Water enters here

Belt driven by Pelton wheel connects to generator

Pelton wheel, also known as the jet-splitting double-bucket turbine (below and right)

HYDROELECTRIC ENERGY

Water turbines like this Pelton wheel are used to produce electricity in hydroelectric power stations. Hydroelectric power is created when the potential energy (pp. 14-15) of water held in a reservoir above a turbine is changed to kinetic energy as the water is released through a nozzle. The water turns a turbine, which is connected to a generator. The rate at which electrical energy is produced depends on how fast the water flows and how far above the turbine the reservoir is. The Pelton wheel was designed by the American mining engineer Lester Pelton (1829-1908).

DUCKS IN THE WATER
As the Sun warms the Earth, it creates wind. The wind's kinetic energy can be changed into electrical energy with the use of wind turbines, which are a development of windmills (pp. 12-13). However, some of the wind's energy disturbs the surface of the sea and causes waves (pp. 40-41), just as blowing over a puddle makes ripples. The waves take some of the wind's kinetic energy, and this energy can be used to generate electricity. One of the most successful ways of doing this is to use Salter Ducks, designed in the 1970s by the British engineer Stephen Salter. Rows of Salter Ducks in the sea absorb much of the energy carried by the waves, and nod up and down as waves hit them. This motion drives pumps that push a liquid through a generator to generate electricity.

USING SALTER DUCKS
Salter Ducks (above right) can be used in oceans, seas, and large lakes. They are attached together and floated in a line so that their pointed "beaks" face incoming waves. Salter Ducks are very efficient, harnessing over one-third of the energy of the waves. Despite this, long lines of them would be needed to generate electricity in quantities large enough to be useful. The design is fairly complex, which means that it may not be practical to use them on a large scale.

Crest of wave

The water moves about a fixed point but does not move along with the wave

WOOD CHIP GAS
Biomass is the name for plants whose energy is made use of by human beings. For instance, logs used for wood-burning stoves are biomass. Small chips of wood can also be used as biomass. The chips are loaded into a tank, where they will be made to produce a gas. This gas is then burned to release its energy. The wood could be used as a fuel itself, but the gas is easier to transport than wood. All the energy stored in the wood chips comes from the Sun and is stored by photosynthesis (pp. 50-51).

PONDS THAT COLLECT ENERGY
Solar energy, or energy from the Sun, can be used directly in many ways. These solar ponds in Israel are an unusual example. The ponds contain a mixture of chemicals that store the Sun's energy. During the winter, this energy is then used to generate cheap electricity. But solar energy can also be used in countries that are not as hot and sunny as Israel. For instance, buildings all over the world use solar collectors to heat water, and solar cells can be used anywhere to operate simple machines like calculators.

ENERGY FROM HOT ROCKS
This power station in Iceland uses geothermal energy, which is heat energy from beneath the surface of the Earth, to produce hot water and steam. The steam drives turbines that generate nearly 3,000,000 J of electrical energy per second, and the hot water is piped to homes. Much of the heat energy comes from molten rocks underground.

Making the most of energy

DURING THE PAST 100 YEARS, the world demand for energy has grown enormously (pp. 56-57). Supplying energy in such huge amounts has caused many problems, such as the limited quantity of fossil fuels (pp. 54-55) available today. Renewable sources of energy (pp. 58-59) can be used as alternatives to fossil fuels, but much more work needs to be done before they can take over. There is one obvious course of action: using less energy. By making the most of the many types of energy that are available, fossil fuels will last longer and alternative energy sources will be further developed. There are many ways of making the most of energy. For example, the energy that public transportation, such as buses and trains, uses is spread between many passengers and can reduce traffic jams in busy cities. Engines designed to be more efficient use less energy to do the same job as other, inefficient, engines. Combined heat and power stations heat water for nearby homes by using heat that would otherwise be wasted. Everyone can help to ensure that energy is used wisely so that there will be plenty left to use in the future.

MAKING THE MOST OF A ROCKING CHAIR
One way to make the most of energy is to use energy that would otherwise be wasted. This "New Domestic Motor," invented in 1873, made use of "the latent feminine energy." It allowed three jobs to be done at once. As the worker rocked in the rocking chair, sewing or doing other handiwork, a system of levers, weights, and pulleys was set in motion. This rocked a baby and churned butter at the same time.

SAME LIGHT, LESS ENERGY
These two light bulbs give out the same amount of light, yet one of them uses much less electrical energy than the other. The meters below show how much electricity is being used each second by the bulbs. The traditional incandescent bulb (pp. 34-35) on the left has a thin, coiled filament that becomes white hot when electricity passes through it. Much of the electricity it uses becomes heat and is wasted. The compact fluorescent bulb (right) has no filament, and much more of the electricity it uses becomes light. A huge amount of energy would be saved if everyone used efficient lighting. Energy can also be saved if lights that are not needed are switched off.

Bulbs produce the same amount of light

60-watt bulb

Incandescent bulb uses over twice the electricity per second as the fluorescent bulb

18-watt bulb

Fluorescent bulb uses much less energy per second than the incandescent bulb

Cable carries electricity

THE SUN CAN HELP

In most countries the Sun is not reliable or powerful enough to provide all the energy a household needs. However, the Sun's energy can be used to supplement other energy sources. Solar collectors like this one, fitted to the roof, can use the Sun's energy to heat water for household use. If the Sun is not intense enough on a particular day, then a gas or electric boiler is used, but on sunnier days the solar collector can supply the needs of a household. The electricity or gas is used only when necessary, and so less energy is wasted.

Pipes hold water for heating

Mineral wool insulates the water pipes

Two layers of metal foil reflect radiant energy back onto water pipes

Light aluminum frame

Transparent film allows radiation from the Sun to be converted into energy

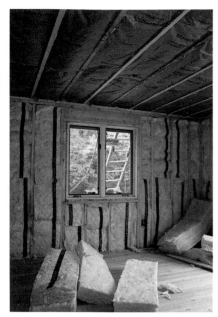

INSULATING THE HOME

Most homes do not use energy efficiently. Heat is lost through windows, walls, and the roof. This means that more energy is needed to keep the house warm. There are many things that can be done to a house to improve its energy efficiency, such as double glazing, draftproofing, and insulating ceilings, walls, floors, and hot-water boilers. Lagging the attic insulates the roof, keeping the house warm in winter and cool in summer. Most modern homes, like this one, are insulated while they are being built, but it is also possible to add insulation to an older home.

SECOND TIME AROUND

This pile of used plastic is waiting to be recycled, rather than being thrown away. To recycle this plastic, it must be heated so that it melts and can be molded into a new shape. Glass (pp. 10-11) can be recycled in a similar way. Recycling is an important way of making the most of energy, because less energy is needed to make things out of recycled materials than if manufacturers start with raw materials. Many people throw things away when they are no longer needed, but this is a waste of the energy that was put into making them, and can cause pollution. Buying fewer unnecessary goods and re-using items are other important ways to be energy efficient.

NEWSPAPER LOGS

Using things again, whether for the same purpose or for something else, can help avoid wasting energy. A good deal of energy can be obtained from many materials by burning them. Some countries burn much of their trash in power stations and use the heat that is released to make steam to power electricity generators. A similar thing can be done on a smaller scale. These logs are made from old newspapers, which are often thrown away after they have been read. Logs like these burn for up to two hours, providing a cheap way to heat a home. Another way paper can be used again is to make it into recycled paper.

Newspapers are soaked in water and placed into this machine to compress them

Compressed and dried newspaper logs

The origins and destiny of energy

T<small>HE</small> U<small>NIVERSE IS TRULY VAST</small>. The Earth is part of the solar system, centered around the Sun. The Sun is one tiny part of a collection of 100,000 million stars in a galaxy called the Milky Way. This is just one of a huge group of galaxies. There are millions upon millions of other galaxies, separated by enormous distances of almost empty space. In that space is the light and other radiation given off by countless stars like the Sun (pp. 48-49). All of the radiation and all of the matter that make up the Universe are forms of energy. At the centers of stars, matter is constantly being lost, but an equivalent amount of energy is always released as a result.

Energy condenses into matter

AN OPEN AND SHUT UNIVERSE
According to Hindu myths, many Universes are created by the god Vishnu when he opens and shuts his eyes. As he opens his eyes, he dreams, and his dream is a new Universe. After many millions of years, he shuts his eyes and that Universe ends. Some scientists believe that the Universe may one day collapse on itself, to be re-born in a new Big Bang. This could repeat forever, with a different Universe resulting each time, just as Vishnu's dreams would each have been different.

The Universe is not infinitely large, but it seems to have begun with a "Big Bang," in which a fixed amount of energy came from nothing. Some scientists say that this fixed amount of energy is available for only a fixed amount of time, and that one day the Universe will be squashed out of existence in a "Big Crunch."

THE BIG BANG
Observations of the stars and galaxies that make up the Universe suggest that they are all moving apart. This means that the very space of which the Universe is made is expanding – stretching like the rubber skin of some huge balloon. If this is true then at some time, about 15,000 million years ago, all of space and time must have come out of nothing in a huge explosion that is now called the Big Bang.

1 SINGLE POINT OF ENERGY
According to the Big Bang theory, all space and time were created at a single point far smaller than an atom. That point must have contained all the energy of the Universe, and because all of space was so small, it must have been incredibly hot. At such high temperatures the forces we know today, such as gravity, would have been very different. There would have been no matter – only heat energy would have existed.

2 A SUDDEN INFLATION OF SPACE
Just after the moment of creation, space and time itself began to expand at an incredible rate. This was not an explosion in space, but an inflation of space. It is thought that the reason for the inflation was that at such high energies, gravity may become a push rather than a pull force.

3 FORMING MATTER
At the end of the very rapid inflation, the Universe became cooler, and the particles that make up matter began to form out of some of the energy. Just as water vapor condenses to form water droplets as it cools, so matter was formed from "condensed" energy as the Universe cooled.

Robert Wilson (left) and Arno Penzias after winning the 1978 Nobel Prize for their discovery

ECHOES OF THE BIG BANG
In 1964 two American physicists, Robert Wilson and Arno Penzias, detected electromagnetic radiation (pp. 40-41), which exactly fitted the predictions of the Big Bang theory. The total amount of energy in the Universe is fixed, and it cannot be destroyed. Much of the energy took the form of matter in the early Universe, but some of it still remains as a "record" of the Big Bang. This record is the radiation that Wilson and Penzias detected.

EXPLORING THE RIPPLES
In 1992 the American COBE (Cosmic Background Explorer) satellite gathered information about the radiation that fills space. When information from the whole sky was put together and enhanced by a computer, it showed that the Universe is not quite the same in every direction. The patches on the picture show that space in the early Universe was not even but contained irregular "ripples," around which energy in the form of matter gathered. This seems to explain why matter is lumped together in some places and not in others.

The Universe continues
to expand

The Universe appears to be flat
but may actually be curved

Between galaxies is
mostly empty space

Galaxies form from
condensing matter

4 **A LUMPY UNIVERSE**
If the Universe was perfectly
smooth as it expanded, it would not
be "lumpy" as it is observed to be. The
young Universe was very slightly irregular,
and gravity pulled together the newly formed
matter into galaxies, which give space its "lumpiness."

5 **CURVED SPACE AND THE END OF TIME**
According to the theory of the Big Bang, the Universe
continues to expand, and this fits with the observation that galaxies
are moving apart. If this theory is correct, space should be "curved" like
the surface of an inflating balloon. From the Earth, space seems to be "flat,"
but it could be very slightly curved, hardly noticeable to us because of the expansion.

Index

Acknowledgments

Dorling Kindersley would like to thank:
John Becklake, Roger Bridgman, Neil Brown, Robert Bud, Clive Bunyan, Ian Carter, Robert Excell, Peter Fitzgerald, Graeme Fyffe, Mike Harding, Emma Hedderwick, Kevin Johnson, John Liffen, Peter Mann, Robert McWilliam, Steve Preston, Fiona Reid, Stephen Roberts, Derek Robinson, John Robinson, Ken Shirt, Victoria Smith, Peter Stephens, Ken Waterman, Jane Wess, Anthony Wilson, David Woodcock, and Michael Wright for advice and help with the provision of objects for photography at the Science Museum; Peter Griffiths for model making; Deborah Rhodes for page make-up; Karl Adamson, Paul Bricknell, Jane Burton and Kim Taylor, Dave King, Tim Ridley, and Jerry Young for additional photography; The British

Museum for photographing the central image on pp. 8-9; Solar Economy, Winchester, UK for providing the cutaway solar panel on p. 61; Peter Wilson, the Ministry of Agriculture, Norwich, for the loan of the calorimeter on p. 53.

Illustrations John Woodcock
Cartography Roger Bullen, James Mills-Hicks
Index Jane Parker

Publisher's note No animal has been injured or in any way harmed during the preparation of this book.

Picture credits

t=top b=bottom c=center l=left r=right

Bettmann Archive 62bl.
Bildarchiv Preussischer Kulturbesitz 30cl.
British Film Institute 41cr; 45cl.

Bulloz 52cr.
Bruce Coleman 48tl; 56tl.
Deutches Museum, Munich 42cl.
Mary Evans Picture Library 7tr; 11tr; 14cl; 18cl; 20tl; 21cr; 30bl; 35tr; 38tl; 41bl; 43tl; 58cl.
Werner Foreman Archive 10tl.
Giraudon 16br.
Robert Harding Picture Library 35br; 61c.
Michael Holford 30tl.
Hulton Deutsche Picture Collection 16tl; 17tl; 24tr; 40cr; 45tr; 48br; 54tr.
Hutchinson Library 10cl.
Image Bank 53c.
© King Features Syndicate Inc. 52tl.
Mansell Collection 9cl.
National Portrait Gallery 22tl.
NASA 31cr; 39cr.
Novosti 44c.
Pelizeus Museum, Hindelsheim 8bl.
Philadelphia Museum of Art, Mr. and Mrs. Wharton Sinkler Collection 19cl.
Planet Earth/Richard Coomer 6bl.
Popperphoto 26bc.
Ann Ronan at Image Select 11tr; 26cl.
Royal Society 24cr.

Professor S. Salter 59tr.
Science Museum Photo Library 12tl; 13cr; 15bl; 29cr; 32cr; 38bl; 39tl; 42tl.
Science Photo Library Keith Kent 6tl; /Stephen Dalton 17tr; /Simon Fraser 33cr; /Oscar Burriel 35bl; /Lecaque/Roussel UCLAF/CNRI 36tl; 40tl; 45tr; /
Los Alamos National Laboratory 46tl; /U.S. Navy 47tr; /Hale Observatory 49tl; /Dr. Ann Smith 52cl; /Lawrence Livermore Laboratory 56cl; /Anthony Howarth 57cr; /U.S. Dept of Energy 59cl; /Simon Fraser 59bl; /NASA 62bc.
York Films of England 56br.
Zefa 47bl; 59cr; 61tl.

With the exception of the items listed above, and objects on pages 6-7; 8-9c; 10-11c; 14b; 15; 16-17cl, c, and br; 19c; 21b and b; 23 tr; 24-25c; 27c; 37; 38-39c; 48-49 bl and c; 51 c and br; 52-53; 54c; 56-57;60-61; 62-63, all the photographs in this book are of objects in the collections of the Science Museum, London.